John Milfull

From Baal to Keuner
The «Second Optimism»
of Bertolt Brecht

Australisch-Neuseeländische Studien zur deutschen Sprache und Literatur

Australian and New Zealand Studies in German Language and Literature

Etudes parues en Australie et Nouvelle Zélande en relation avec la philologie Allemande

herausgegeben von
Gerhard Schulz (Melbourne)
und John A. Asher (Auckland)

Bd. 5

John Milfull

From Baal to Keuner
The «Second Optimism»
of Bertolt Brecht

Herbert Lang
Bern and Frankfurt/M.
1974

John Milfull

From Baal to Keuner

The «Second Optimism» of Bertolt Brecht

Herbert Lang
Bern and Frankfurt/M.
1974

ISBN 3 261 01015 0

© Herbert Lang & Co. Ltd., Bern (Switzerland)
Peter Lang Ltd., Frankfurt/M. (West-Germany)
1974. All rights reserved.

Printed by Lang Druck Ltd., Liebefeld/Berne (Switzerland)

FROM BAAL TO KEUNER

The "Second Optimism" of Bertolt Brecht

by

JOHN MILFULL

CONTENTS

FOREWORD

This book is the revised version of a thesis submitted in March, 1967 for the degree of Doctor of Philosophy at the University of Sydney, Australia. My thanks are due to Professor Lawrence Ryan for his help and criticism over a number of years; to the University of New South Wales, the Alexander von Humboldt-Stiftung and the Australian Research Grants Committee, who all contributed towards the study period in Berlin which enabled me to correct, revise and expand the original version; to the Bertolt-Brecht-Archiv, for permission to consult unpublished material; to Dr. Reiner Steinweg, without whose assistance I should have been able to make little use of it; and to the many colleagues, students and other friends with whom I have discussed the subject over the past few years.

Sydney, January 1973

INTRODUCTION

When Brecht died in 1956, his reputation rested mainly on the plays which he had written during the years of emigration and brought to the stage in such perfection after his return to East Berlin. It was only natural that these works and their attendant theoretical writings should have become the starting-point for the wave of critical studies which followed; together, they seemed to form a "canon" of unusual completeness and direct relevance to the problems of contemporary society and its theatre. The "early Brecht," like so many of his Expressionist contemporaries, seemed almost forgotten, and when he was "rediscovered," it was often only in order to "prove" that his later political and aesthetic ideas had been present in his work in a "primitive" form from the beginning. It is only over the last few years that the early work has begun to be appreciated and studied in its own right; once again, the theatre led the way with productions of the early plays which needed no historical excuses to justify them. There are even signs that the "Lehrstücke" of the middle period, which had found few friends in the first flush of the Brecht cult, are finally being restored to their rightful place in his life's work.[1]

Despite all this new interest in the earlier Brecht, there have been few attempts to arrive at a more "organic" understanding of his artistic development. Esslin's biography[2] virtually disqualifies itself by its political bias and its high-handed refusal to verify intuition through research; Marxist critics are loth to venture onto the somewhat perilous terrain of the early works, and the few works which consider Brecht's *oeuvre* as a whole are generally limited by their concentration on a particular aspect of his technique or his philosophy, rather than on his total development as a writer. More specialised studies tend to be partisan, to defend the early Brecht against the later and *vice versa,* while the old summary division into "Pre-Marxist" and "Marxist" phases still rages unchecked in many areas. Yet it seems obvious that we can only fully understand Brecht's development after 1930 if we can see it as a logical consequence of the position he had reached in the last "Pre-Marxist" works, and that the temptation to "back-interpret," to apply the categories of the later work to the earlier and to see only what they would have us see, to which Brecht himself was by no means immune, must be firmly resisted.

The following abbreviations are used in the footnotes:
GW = Bertolt Brecht, *Gesammelte Werke,* Werkausgabe edition suhrkamp, 20 vols., Frankfurt 1967
BBA = Bertolt Brecht Archiv, followed by number of "Mappe" and "Blatt"

---

[1] cf. especially Reiner Steinweg, *Das Lehrstück. Brechts Theorie einer politisch-ästhetischen Erziehung,* Stuttgart 1971
[2] Martin Esslin, *Brecht. Das Paradox des politischen Dichters,* Frankfurt 1962

It would seem that a more defensible and "organic" approach would be to begin our investigation with an independent study of the early works which abandons this anticipatory method and concentrates severely on the works in hand and the contemporary source material, on what "is" there rather than on what "ought to be" there. Any such re-interpretation will inevitably affect our understanding of Brecht's development after 1930, indeed, it would seem that until we are able to see the two "halves" of Brecht's work in their full and complex relationship, the conclusions we draw about either are likely to be questionable. We must find the "continuity within the change."

To speak of two "halves" is, however, not to exaggerate the abruptness of the change which seems to confront us in Brecht's work in the years 1929–30. *Das Badener Lehrstück vom Einverständnis* and *Die heilige Johanna der Schlachthöfe* are a far cry from Brecht's earlier dramatic practice, which reaches an end-point in *Aufstieg und Fall der Stadt Mahagonny*. A similar change is obvious in Brecht's verse; the *Sonette*[3] of the late twenties mark the end of a development as clearly as *Mahagonny* — the new poetry is impersonal, politically orientated and heavily disciplined. Here, however, the two styles tend to overlap in a way which can be seen in the plays perhaps only in the *Fatzer*-fragment. Brecht himself stressed the more "private" character of his poetry, and in the absence of letters and diaries, it becomes of fundamental importance in tracing his development in these years. Of course, any such "chronological" approach is severely hampered by the extraordinary editorial policy adopted by Suhrkamp and by the enormous difficulties involved in dating much of the material — yet the attempt must be made. Whether or not this editorial attitude has its roots in Brecht's own personal reserve in the later years and his desire "die Spuren zu verwischen," or even in his life-long antipathy to *Literaturwissenschaft,* it is clear that as long as it persists, there is little hope of reaching a real understanding of the central "crisis" in his literary and political career. Brecht's craving for anonymity may have been understandable in his lifetime (if not always entirely convincing), but to perpetuate it through clumsy and misleading editions of his work seems absurd. "Das Heute geht gespeist durch das Gestern in das Morgen,"[4] and to understand and evaluate his conclusions we must know how he reached them.

Despite these difficulties, it is clear that this "crisis" must remain the central concern of any serious attempt to understand Brecht's development as a writer. For the present, we shall restrict ourselves largely to insights gained from the works themselves, a procedure which must necessarily run the risk of seeming sometimes rather speculative in character. However, the method of "back-interpretation" criticised above seems really to be on no more solid ground,

---

3 GW 8, pp. 160–165
4 *Bei Durchsicht meiner ersten Stücke,* GW 17, p. 952

particularly when it bases its approach on Brecht's own distancing of himself from the works of the early period. This, it seems reasonable to assume, was at least partly an attempt to conceal, discredit or transform those "remains" which had survived the "great purge" of the thirties, a purge which can only be understood as a reaction to the ideas and conclusions of the younger Brecht, and, in a particular sense, as their logical consequence.

By 1930, Brecht was a convinced Marxist and had embarked on a process which was to engage him constantly throughout the rest of his life: the attempt to "transform" — "umfunktionieren" — as he had so successfully done with Galy Gay, the early Brecht into a "new" Marxist Brecht and to strip him of all the "irrelevant" personal traits which were now undesirable. It is not altogether surprising that some of these explanations smack rather of the virtue of the reformed drunkard; more serious is their tendency to assume the form of a deliberate self-denial, a sometimes rather unsuccessful attempt to prove himself wrong. A number of the conclusions he had reached were, however, of such validity and consequence that he seems to have found it difficult, even impossible, to "repeal" them. As Friedrich Dürrenmatt later wrote, "Was einmal gedacht wurde, kann nicht mehr zurückgenommen werden."[5]

This attempted "Zurücknahme" is nowhere more obvious than in the two last plays of the early period, *Aufstieg und Fall der Stadt Mahagonny* and *Die Dreigroschenoper*. Over the latter Brecht became involved in a long court case; having sold the film rights, he demanded such drastic changes in the social "working-out" of the opera that it could only have been a failure with the bourgeois who had loved it on stage. So much did the "wrong success" of this work pre-occupy Brecht that he re-worked the material twice, in the film scenario *Die Beule* and in the novel *Der Dreigroschenroman*. It seems, in fact, to have been a major factor in precipitating Brecht's "conversion"; the realisation that its extreme nihilism could be accepted and even enjoyed as "harmless" by the society he detested seems to have driven him to more positive forms of protest. (Peter Weiss has reacted in a not dissimilar way to the world-wide success of *Marat/Sade*.) *Aufstieg und Fall der Stadt Mahagonny* was, as we shall see, not only substantially revised and altered for publication in 1930 — it seems to represent for Brecht a position whose untenability itself formed the pivot of this "change."

Mahagonny is, for a number of reasons, a key work in the development of the younger Brecht. In it, the themes and pre-occupations of the early work are presented with a high degree of conciseness and in their most developed form, which makes it an excellent starting-point for an investigation of the change which came over Brecht's work in the early thirties. We shall see that its origins date back to the early days in München, and that Brecht was concerned with its

5 *Die Physiker*, Möbius's last speech

revisions as late as 1930 — it thus spans the entire early period. Further, *Mahagonny* still observes a convention which we shall see to be typical of the early work as a whole: that of the "open hero," who stands rather unambiguously for the author and whose relationship to the society about him is the fundamental concern of the play. Jimmy Mahony is a direct descendant of Baal; Galy Gay and Macheath no longer belong to this type, they anticipate the later Brechtian protagonist, the "Versuchskarnickel" upon whom the thesis is demonstrated, who "knows" less than the author.

My method, then, has been to trace the dominant themes of the early work to their final consequence in *Mahagonny*. The position reached there I have regarded as the "negative pole" throughout the period of crisis, and have therefore analysed it in considerable detail.

In the second chapter the crisis itself is considered. Here again I have tried to demonstrate the "poles" of the argument with reference to *Das Badener Lehrstück vom Einverständnis,* the two fragments *Untergang des Egoisten Johann Fatzer* and *Der böse Baal der asoziale* and the *Geschichten vom Herrn Keuner.* The two fragments are of exemplary importance, for in them, as we shall see, Brecht confronts the *alter ego* of his first period, Baal/Fatzer, with a figure who was to assume a similar position in the later work, Herr Keuner. In an analysis of this opposition and of the Keuner figure I hope to find the clue to the "transformation" in Brecht's work, and to relate it to the problem of "loss of identity" in the first Marxist plays. The chapter is "framed" by short analyses of *Mann ist Mann* and *Die heilige Johanna,* which aim to show how this problem derives from the early work and what solutions it was later to find.

In the final chapter I have attempted to illustrate the survival of these problems in the later plays and poems. Brecht's "second optimism,"[6] as I have termed it, is the result of a precarious balance. The negative pole of *Mahagonny* persists in the later work, even if it is no longer expressed directly; it acts as a control gainst which any "positive" qualities must first assert themselves. We shall see that the conclusions of *Mahagonny* could never be more than partially "taken back" by Brecht, and thus arrive at the "continuity within the change."

---

[6] cf. Konrad Farner, "Über die Weisheit in unserm Zeitalter," *Sinn und Form,* 2. Sonderheft Bertolt Brecht, Berlin 1957, p. 117

CHAPTER ONE

I

Among Brecht's dramatic projects in 1926 was a series of plays under the general title "Einzug der Menschheit in die großen Städte."[1] It is a recurrent theme in his early work, even to the extent that he remodelled his own life-story to fit in with it in the poem "Vom armen B. B.," which appeared as an "Anhang" to the *Hauspostille,* Brecht's first collection of verse, in 1927. The "black forests" of "Vom armen B. B.," from which his mother "bore him within her body," may, like the "Asphaltstadt" (Augsburg!) be something of a poetic licence, but they form perhaps the commonest opposition in his early plays and poems. Baal and Ekart revolt against the "city" and play out their tragedy in a world of forests and rivers. Garga's family in *Im Dickicht der Städte* comes "aus dem flachen Land" to Chicago, a similar motif, and the dénouement of the play takes place "im Gestrüpp" on the banks of Lake Michigan. In *Mahagonny* there is the same contrast between the "black forests" of Alaska and the "Paradies-stadt," and even Kragler in *Trommeln in der Nacht* seems often to be returning from the country rather than from the war. In the early poetry, we are confronted mainly by "nature" poems, in which the commonest landscape is a dense, primaeval forest, and by "city" poems, where the "naked animal" in man struggles with a new and hostile environment. In a very real sense, Marie Farrar and Jakob Apfelböck are "animals" whose instinctive processes have been thrown into disorder by their new environment. As Bronnen writes, "Der Kleinstädter Brecht [wurde] mit dem Problem der Millionenstadt nie fertig."[2]

Brecht's early heroes, of whom Baal is the archetype, have lost an original unity with nature, to which, in the end, they return. In *Baal* and in "Vom armen B. B." this sense of a lost original unity is related to a clearly expressed regressive yearning:

> O ihr, die ihr aus Himmel und Hölle vertrieben!
> Ihr Mörder, denen viel Leides geschah!
> Warum seid ihr nicht im Schoß eurer Mütter geblieben,
> Wo es stille war und man schlief und war da?[3]

The search for this "oneness" is a hopeless one; in the world of the "Asphaltstädte," into which he has been "verschlagen," Brecht can see it only in the pre-natal, unconscious existence or in day-dream images of a far-away, Rousseauish existence in the face of nature in its more aggressive forms — the

---

[1] Elisabeth Hauptmann, "Notizen über Brechts Arbeit 1926," *Sinn und Form,* 2. Sonderheft Bertolt Brecht, p. 243

[2] Arnolt Bronnen, *Tage mit Bert Brecht,* Munich 1960, p. 47

[3] GW 1, p. 60

"sieben Jahre in Alaska" of *Mahagonny,* a world of male camaraderie under intense hardship, which appears again and again in the early poems and short stories, a world which vacillates between Kipling and Karl May on the one hand and Rimbaud and Verlaine on the other. As a "vagrant," Baal feels himself again at one with the world about him, "der Himmel . . . deckte mächtig seine Blöße zu."

In this "masculine" world, life is difficult, but moments of exaltation are still possible. The dream of a possible existence which Baal tries to realise with Ekart is destroyed by women, who represent for Brecht at this stage the settled petrifaction of bourgeois security. Baal's callousness is, above all, an attempt to ward off the demands being made on him, the desire of his mistresses to "hold him," to impose a stasis on him (a variant of the Don Juan theme). Yet he is driven by a kind of alcoholic/sexual fatalism, an *amor fati,* to experience everything; his excesses are due to a kind of inspired impatience, a desire to hasten the end of an inevitable progression from "Mutterschoß" to "Erden-schoß" (Perhaps Don Juan, too, is not unrelieved to welcome his "stone guest" — he also seems well on the way to exhausting his own possibilities!). The entire "Choral vom großen Baal" is dominated by the image of the "Schoß"; life becomes a constant attempt to regain a womb-like feeling of "Geborgenheit":

> Und das große Weib Welt, das sich lachend gibt
> Dem, der sich zermalmen läßt von ihren Knien
> Gab ihm einige Ekstase, die er liebt
> Aber Baal starb nicht: er sah nur hin.
>
> Und wenn Baal nur Leichen um sich sah
> War die Wollust immer doppelt groß.
> Man hat Platz, sagt Baal, es sind nicht viele da.
> Man hat Platz in dieses Weibes Schoß.[4]

Sexuality itself becomes an expression of the desire to attain the oneness of the "Mutterschoß," but it is rejected for its failure to "absorb" Baal completely. The feeling of physical separation, the *omne animal post coitum triste* becomes an echo of the separation of birth. Baal and Ekart share this experience, and try to escape from sexuality into a wider image of the desired condition, "die große Welt," Gaea herself, in whom all matter, dead or alive, is carried. The poem "Vom ertrunkenen Mädchen"[5] is the most perfect expression of Baal/Brecht's fascination with this state of pre-conscious unity, and its imagery recurs constantly in the other works of the period. Ekart's summons to Baal on their first meeting in the "Branntweinschenke," for all its exaggerated pathos, is close to the centre of the play:

4 GW 1, p. 3
5 GW 8, p. 252

Zu den Kuhställen, wo man zwischen Tieren schläft: sie sind finster und voll
vom Gemuhe der Kühe. Und zu den Wäldern, wo das erzene Schallen oben ist
und man das Licht des Himmels vergißt: Gott hat einen vergessen . . .[6]

Instead of the conscious, "light" transcendence of the divine totality Brecht
demands a "dark" totality of matter, without mind or consciousness.

The inspired alliance of Baal and Ekart fails when Ekart relapses into
sexuality, more out of pity than desire. Yet Ekart's pity seems only a projection
of the pity that Baal himself is trying to strangle: "Die Kellnerin hat die Züge
Sophiens." Baal's "callousness" is at once a camouflage for his own sensitivity
and the result of a basic disgust with his own "uncleanness," a determination not
to "wash himself"[7] or any of the things around him, to see them in their natural
faecality. This sensitivity which finds itself attacked on all sides, which can find
no proper "food," like Kafka's "Hungerkünstler," rejects itself for a masochistic
heightening of the "uncleanness" of self and world, rejects the "light" for the
"dark," transcendence for "nothingness." Regression becomes self-destructive,
the impossibility of the desired ideal leads to the destruction of the real, the self.
Throughout the early poems we find a fascination with the progress of this
self-destruction, even to the extent of a consciousness of physical decay in the
body of the poet himself.[8] Sexuality, too, becomes part of this "Selbstvernichtungsprozeß" — Frau Peachum's aggressive little song in Die Dreigroschenoper points a moral which has been forming in Brecht's mind for years: "Und
sogar er beginnt nun zu verstehn / daß ihm des Weibes Loch das Grabloch war."[9]

For Brecht, this process has all the attraction and all the repulsion of a closed
development. "Vernichtung" has its inevitable end, in "Nichts." This realisation
is expressed perhaps most clearly in an early poem, significantly entitled "Der
Nachgeborene":

> Ich gestehe es: ich
> Habe keine Hoffnung.
> Die Blinden reden von einem Ausweg. Ich
> Sehe.
>
> Wenn die Irrtümer verbraucht sind
> Sitzt als letzter Gesellschafter
> Uns das Nichts gegenüber.[10]

---

[6] GW 1, p. 16
[7] cf. "Die Achillesverse," GW 8, p. 53
[8] cf. "Vom schlechten Gebiß," GW 8, p. 48, and "Gesang von einer Geliebten," GW 8,
p. 78
[9] GW 2, p. 461
[10] GW 8, p. 99. One may perhaps be forgiven for a slight scepticism about Brecht's
own comment on this poem, "eines der ältesten Gedichte aus der Frühzeit" (GW 10, p. 5*);
it would be hard to support on stylistic grounds. Perhaps he is using "alt" in the same sense
as Herr Keuner in "Das Altertum" (GW 12, p. 388)?

It is not easy to reconcile the complete finality of this poem with the guarded optimism of the later years. It leaves us waiting for the "end of time," the finite end to the narrowing "gyres" of the "Selbstvernichtungsprozeß." In the later "Sonett über schlechtes Leben," Brecht expresses this "end-state" even more directly:

> Ich haucht' in meine Hand schon hinterm Spind
> Und roch an meinem Atem: da roch er faulig.
>
> Da sagt ich zu mir selbst: ich sterbe bald.
> Seitdem bemerk ich ohne Lust und kalt
> Wie langsam mir die kurze Zeit verrinnt.[11]

(It is no coincidence that these lines are given to Fatzer in the *Fatzer*-fragment and that they are echoed in the "Austreibung" of the *Badener Lehrstück,* as we shall see.) He is unable to postulate any further development after the end of the "waiting" has been reached — "es kommt nichts nachher." The individual death which is the finite, slowly-approaching end-point of the "Sonett" brings, in *Mahagonny,* the end of the world order with it; this is already implied in "Der Nachgeborene," where the "way out" is by definition a way both for individual and society, since for Brecht an "individual" solution *à la* Rilke is impossible and meaningless — from the first his characters are pre-occupied with the search for a "Land, wo es besser zu leben ist," a society in which it is no longer necessary for them to be "destroyed" in this way. Baal's inability to find a possible *modus vivendi* between the original unity of the unborn and the "uncivilised" and the end in the "dunkler Erdenschoß" forces him to become, as Brecht later puts it, "asozial . . . in einer asozialen Gesellschaft."[12] The problem remains, in the last analysis, a social one.

At this stage, Brecht denies the possibility of such a "way out," for himself or for others. In "Vom armen B. B." he writes succinctly:

> Von diesen Städten wird bleiben: der durch sie
>   hindurchging, der Wind!
> Fröhlich machet das Haus den Esser: er leert es.
> Wir wissen, daß wir Vorläufige sind
> Und nach uns wird kommen: nichts Nennenswertes.[13]

(Compare Fatzer's "mir scheint, ich bin vorläufig, aber was / läuft nach? "[14]) It is important to stress the seriousness of this universal pessimism. Critics may perhaps be forgiven for failing to see the full tragic banality of *Mahagonny*

11 GW 8, p. 164
12 *Bei Durchsicht meiner ersten Stücke,* GW 17, p. 947
13 GW 8, p. 262
14 BBA 109/17

behind its "culinary" trappings, but it is irresponsible to neglect the extra-ordinary directness and consistency of Brecht's poetry at this time and to shrug it off, as so many are inclined to do, as "irrelevant" to the later Brecht.

It is not difficult to trace the development of this "pessimism" from *Baal* to *Mahagonny*. Already in *Trommeln in der Nacht* the "hero," Kragler, is so convinced of the futility of attempting to stem this self-destructive process that he adopts, as Brecht later shamefacedly admits, "die schäbigste aller möglichen Varianten ... er bekommt sein Mädchen zurück, wenn auch beschädigt, und kehrt der Revolution den Rücken."[15] "Das große, weiße, breite Bett" that follows is Kragler's "Grabloch"; love has become a "Sterbesakrament." Kragler, like B. B., pictures himself as "mißtrauisch und faul und zufrieden am End," but this "Zufriedenheit" is clearly not forthcoming; it is a half-hearted attempt to smile at the approaching "Nichts." Characteristically, he wishes to destroy the "theatre," to pull the world crashing about his ears, yet at the same time to escape into his private forgetting. When he raves at the audience in the final scene, it is not "Verfremdung"; Kragler wants to "go home" as they do, having written off the reality of his predicament as "theatre."

The human contact which, despite everything, is still possible in *Baal* and *Trommeln in der Nacht* has, in *Im Dickicht der Städte*, itself become problematical. Baal and Ekart are still able to communicate, Kragler pre-supposes a host of fellow-Kraglers, but Garga and Shlink are forced to realise that even enmity has become impossible: "die unendliche Vereinzelung des Menschen macht eine Feindschaft zum unerreichbaren Ziel."[16] In their final dialogue, Brecht destroys even Kragler's last illusion; Garga, who escapes, as Shlink puts it, "mit dem nackten Leben in der Tasche," has only the Mahagonny of New York to look forward to. A Kragler-like attempt at forgetting is no longer possible — Garga is left, like the "Nachgeborene," "dem Nichts gegenüber," waiting pointlessly. The final words of the play mark an "end-point" as clearly as the "Sonett über schlechtes Leben":

> Allein sein ist eine gute Sache. Das Chaos ist aufgebraucht.
> Es war die beste Zeit.[17]

In 1922 Brecht admitted to Bronnen that the "Aussage" of the play was contained in this "letzter Satz" — it represented for him a "new consciousness." Yet Bronnen sees in the play "Embryologie, Stammesgeschichte der Familie Brecht, zusammen mit unverdaut ausgeschiedenen individualistischen Resten" and denies *Im Dickicht* this "final" character:

---

[15] *Bei Durchsicht meiner ersten Stücke,* p. 945
[16] GW 1, p. 187
[17] GW 1, p. 193

es [das Werk] blieb lange für ihn ein Chaos, und lange sah er gegenüber dem
Chaos keine anderen Möglichkeiten, als es "aufzubrauchen."[18]

We shall see later that this pre-occupation of Brecht's with his own "autobio-
graphy" and his attempts to "conclude" it persists into the first Marxist plays
and that it is only there that a "solution" is found. For all Brecht's manifest
desire to drive the "Selbstvernichtungsprozeß" to its conclusion, it remained the
basic concern of his work right up till *Mahagonny*, where "chaos" is no longer
primarily a personal experience, as in *Im Dickicht*, but has invaded all levels of
society. The point of consciousness attained in Garga's last speech gives way to
an even more acute realisation of the "end-state":

> Wo immer du hingehst
> Es nützt nichts.
> Wo du auch seist
> Du entrinnst nicht.
> Am besten wird es sein
> Du bleibst sitzen
> Und wartest auf das Ende.[19]

Brecht's experience of time in these works comes remarkably close to the
static consciousness to be found in so many of Samuel Beckett's works, the
consciousness of Vladimir and Estragon, of Hamm and Clov, that they have
already exhausted all possibilities of action, meaningful and meaningless, that
they have truly come to the "end," and yet the end refuses to come to them, it
leaves them waiting in a state of absurd and hopeless immobility. In the title of
the latter play, *Fin de Partie,* Beckett finds perhaps the best image of all for this
state: "end-game," the stage of the game of chess where neither player has the
dominance to achieve clear results, where the game degenerates into a slow and
painful attempt to avert a draw or a stalemate — and at the same time, a true
"end-game," the game of those who have come to the end but have found an
empty space before them, between them and the true, unattainable end, which
must be filled in by "play," however meaningless it may be, simply out of the
necessity to do something. Thus the actions of Beckett's characters are without
meaning, all meaning has already been exhausted, and yet the rituals continue,
the games with hats and chairs and trees. Godot and the end of time fail to
arrive.

From *Im Dickicht der Städte* on, Brecht is possessed by the sensation that no
further development is possible, that he is already on the "brink" of the end of
time, that a point of maximum chaos has been reached which can only be

---

18 Bronnen, op.cit., p. 47, pp. 133ff.
19 GW 2, p. 525

followed by a gradual gyrating towards the end. The impatience, the boredom with this "closed development" leads him to attempt in each successive work to advance the "brink" still further, to force time to stop. On the other hand, he is faced with the realisation "wie langsam mir die kurze Zeit verrinnt." The "end" which has been sensed and accepted refuses to make its appearance, like Godot, and leaves the poet in a kind of perpetual asymptosis. The progression is that of a spiral which never reaches its centre. As Ross Chambers writes in an essay on "Beckett's Brinkmanship" (to which I am indebted for its analysis of this "end-state"):

> And so we are condemned finally to be always tantalisingly on a kind of threshold, always close to stepping out of time and space into our selves, but never quite able to do so, for at each step our object recedes, revealing yet another step to be taken. Our existence seems to have reached the furthest point to which we can take it, it is to all intents and purposes over, and yet it is still going on. And it *must* go on, for it has not attained its end, the end which is unattainable.[20]

This "receding of the object, revealing another step to be taken" which is so characteristic of Beckett's work is one of the basic experiences of the world of *Im Dickicht* and *Mahagonny*. At the same time, Brecht's desire to escape from this progression is less metaphysical than Beckett's — the moment of release, "outside time and space," has for Brecht only a negative meaning, in the destruction of an unendurable consciousness. There is no real desire for the "silence of eternal self-possession"; he wishes rather to re-establish the silence that was there at the beginning, before consciousness, before birth. The possibility of attaining this freedom through or in art, which Beckett both accepts and rejects, is for Brecht out of the question. From the beginning he violently opposes all attempts to set up a "further" existence in art; his work is the expression of an almost religious materialism, for which art is strictly utilitarian, designed to give entertainment and instruction, to show the world "as it is" and to become itself "reality." Unlike Beckett, he is unable to advance a reason, other than compulsion, for continuing on this path towards the end; for him it brings only the "Nichts," there is no question of "stirb und werde," but merely ceasing to be. Beckett's attempts to advance the "brink" are justified by his sensing beyond it a release which is in itself a higher state of being; to Brecht, the end is only a "way out," an escape into not-being. Once he has become aware of this progression, he is forced increasingly to negate the value of any action, whether in "reality" or art. He has no "reason" to continue to present its successive stages in his work, since, as he admits, it leads nowhere. In terms of "Der Nachgeborene," the destruction of all illusions itself becomes an illusion, a

---

[20] Ross Chambers, "Beckett's Brinkmanship," *AUMLA*, No. 19 (May 1963), p. 61

false "way out," since life and art cannot "overtake" it. The "chaos" can never be "used up" because "das Nichts" is unattainable, as Beckett was later to find in *L'Innommable*. Nor is history prepared to oblige Brecht with the apocalypse which he seems to demand of it in the works of this period; the "short time" of waiting refuses to take an end.

It is not, then, altogether surprising to find Brecht in 1926 already concerned with "der neue Mensch";[21] the desire to escape from this sense of "waiting," of pointlessness, runs as an undercurrent through the early plays and poems. We have already seen how Baal and his counterparts in the early poems have visions of a "Utopia," an often remote and mythical country "wo es besser zu leben ist." In *Im Dickicht der Städte* Garga has a similar plan to escape to Tahiti; Mahagonny itself is a Utopia gone wrong. The alternative to such an escape, whose possibility is now rejected, is to change the individual in such a way that he can again be "fitted in" to society. This is, of course, only the preliminary stage of a realisation on Brecht's part that both individual and society must be changed; yet in *Mann ist Mann* and *Die Dreigroschenoper* he pursues it to consequences which contrast oddly with the humanism of the later work. Galy Gay and Macheath solve the problem by taking society on its own terms; for them "das Wachstum im Kollektiv" becomes a "Wachstum ins Verbrecherische."[22] Although Brecht later saw the problem of *Mann ist Mann* as "das falsche, schlechte Kollektiv (der "Bande") und seine Verführungskraft, jenes Kollektiv, das in diesen Jahren Hitler und seine Geldgeber rekrutierten, das unbestimmte Verlangen der Kleinbürger nach dem geschichtlich reifen, echten sozialen Kollektiv der Arbeiter ausbeutend,"[23] his sympathy lies at this stage explicitly with Galy Gay and implicitly with Macheath. (We shall examine Brecht's attempted "Zurücknahme" of *Mann ist Mann* in Chapter Two.) As he writes in "Das zehnte Sonett":

> Was ich nicht gern gesteh: gerade ich
> Verachte solche, die im Unglück sind.[24]

It is the capacity of his two heroes to adapt themselves to the world around them, their "success," which Brecht cannot help admiring. *Mann ist Mann* presents in a curiously negative form the process of survival by adapting oneself to one's surroundings which was to be one of Brecht's main concerns in his later work. Macheath and Jimmy Mahony/Paul Ackermann are less successful than Galy Gay; Paul is destroyed by his loyalty to Joe, and Macheath falls victim to "die sexuelle Hörigkeit" and can only be saved by a *deux ex machina*. Galy has

---

21   cf. E. Hauptmann, op.cit., p. 242
22   *Bei Durchsicht meiner ersten Stücke,* p. 951
23   loc.cit.
24   GW 8, p. 164

succeeded in removing the obstacle that stands in their way: personality. As we shall see, he is a strange anticipation of the "kleinste Größe" of the thirties, but as yet oddly neutral in character. In a sense, *Mann ist Mann* already shows the possibility of "der neue Mensch," but the new society into which he is to be integrated is still missing. It stands outside the main development of the early work, looking forward rather than back. It is significant that *Mahagonny,* which returns so clearly to the "alter Mensch" and the old society, should have been written after it.

Die Dreigroschenoper remains less important for its intrinsic qualities than for the effect its success with the bourgeoisie had on Brecht's thinking. It is clear that he and Weill regarded it as something of a pot-boiler, an interruption to their serious work on *Mahagonny;* indeed, in *Happy End* they even attempted the same thing again. The comparison between capitalists and robbers on which Brecht's re-working of the original *Beggar's Opera* material is based seems facile and over-simplified when we compare it with the analysis of society in *Mahagonny.* In *Die Dreigroschenoper* Brecht is dealing with a "manufactured" plot which, with the speed of composition, tends to restrict his movements. It is no coincidence that the songs, specifically detached from the dialogue, are on an altogether more personal level, despite all borrowings. They fit easily into the pattern of his "confessional" verse; despite the incidental revolutionary rumblings of the "Lied der Seeräuber-Jenny,"[25] the fatalism of the early poems dominates, in its usual forms: sex, alcohol and fisticuffs. When Brecht came to re-work the material later for *Der Dreigroschenroman,* he found it necessary to make extensive changes, not merely in the "execution," but in the "Fabel" itself. It is by no means surprising that the bourgeoisie were so taken by the opera in its original form, with its often undisguised "outlaw-romanticism"; they were, no doubt, flattered to find themselves compared to the elegant and fashionably cynical robber-captain Macheath, especially as in the process of proving his theorem about robbers and bourgeois Brecht had turned him into a very respectable robber indeed, one who would not stoop to do the unpleasant work himself (he solved the problem more adequately in the characterisation of Pierpont Mauler). The burlesque of the opera provides a stylisation which enables the audience to ignore the "moral" or to alter its "function" in their own way.

In *Aufstieg und Fall der Stadt Mahagonny,* such a misunderstanding is no longer possible. The provocation which in *Die Dreigroschenoper* misfires to some extent because of its essential lack of seriousness is conveyed in *Mahagonny* with a violent directness. The "stylisation" of *Dreigroschenoper* is replaced by an "intentional ugliness," a baldness of style which testifies to the nearness of the

---

[25] cf. Ernst Bloch, "Lied der Seeräuber-Jenny," *Bertolt Brechts Dreigroschenbuch,* Frankfurt 1960, pp. 195—197

"Lehrstücke" and which leaves us in no doubt as to the seriousness of the intended provocation. This opera "sägt schon am alten Ast,"[26] as Brecht writes in the *Anmerkungen,* in more than one sense, and more than "a little"; when the branch falls at the end, the sawer falls with it. It is in this work that Brecht drives his pessimism, his aggressive impatience with the "waiting for the end" we have seen in the works of the early period to such an extreme that it leads to an "Umschlag." The position reached in *Mahagonny* is so final that to continue beyond it means virtually to make a fresh start. To understand this "Umschlag," we can do no better than to analyse in detail the structure and content of this last of his early works, seeing in it a more or less schematic representation of his progress from *Baal* to the "toter Punkt" of 1928—29.

II

The origins of *Mahagonny* are complex in the extreme. The five "Mahagonny-gesänge" which form the germ of the later opera seem to have their roots in the München of the early twenties, although they were not published until 1926, in the *Taschenpostille;* Arnolt Bronnen tells us of Brecht's invention of the term "Mahagonny" in 1923, under the influence of Nazi demonstrators, "diese Masse braunbehemdeter Kleinbürger . . . , hölzerne Gestalten mit ihrer falsch einge-färbten, durchlöcherten Fahne":

> Der Begriff wuchs ihm aus dem Wort, wandelte sich mit ihm; doch in jenem Sommer 1923 mochte er ihm zunächst Spießers Utopia bedeuten, jenen zynisch-dummen Stammtisch-Staat, der aus Anarchie und Alkohol die bis dahin gefährlichste Mixtur für Europas Hexenkessel zusammenbraute.[27]

It seems probable that the "Gesänge" date from this period. Their publication attracted the attention of Kurt Weill, who approached Brecht for permission to set them to music. Brecht agreed and added a "Finale," "Aber dieses ganze Mahagonny . . ." and a number of "Zwischensprüche." It was in this form, with orchestral interludes, that the work was first performed in Baden-Baden in 1927 as the so-called "Songspiel" *Mahagonny.* It was, however, immediately with-drawn, as Weill had already conceived the idea of a "large-scale tragic opera" on the same theme.[28]

At the time, Brecht was engaged — apparently simultaneously — on a quite bewildering number of dramatic projects, which, however, show a close relationship in theme. In a period "die vom einzug der menschheit in die großen

---

26 cf. GW 17, p. 1016
27 Bronnen, op.cit., p. 143—4
28 cf. David Drew, "The History of Mahagonny," *Musical Times* 1963/1, pp. 18—24

städte erfüllt wird,"[29] the great cities, "die für unzerstörbare galten,"[30] Brecht is possessed by apocalyptic visions of a new "Sintflut," which will destroy these cities and the corrupt society which dwells in them. The disastrous Florida hurricane of 1926 came to have an exemplary, symbolic significance for him; it is, I think, no coincidence that the mass of newspaper cuttings and other material which Brecht assembled for a projected play entitled *Der Untergang der Paradiesstadt Miami,* which has some claim to being considered as an "Ur-*Mahagonny*," should be mingled, in the folder in which it is contained in the Brecht Archive,[31] with fragments of *Die Sintflut,* one of the most characteristic projects of this period. Indeed, the boundaries between the two works are ill-defined; from the following quotation we might well assume that the *Miami* material was to be absorbed into *Die Sintflut:*

> Untergegangen ist die Großstadt Gomorrha
> Seit gestern ist der große Hafen Jokohama nur mehr Wasser
> Heute früh verschwand die Paradiesstadt Miami
> Und nicht mehr antwortet jetzt das gewaltige Sodom.[32]

Had Brecht completed *Die Sintflut,* it would have become the bleakest and most apocalyptic of all his plays. The "Weltuntergang" which is foreshadowed in "Vom armen B. B." is here carried out with the utmost thoroughness. The central figure of the play, the prophet Nahaia, calls for this destruction as the logical end of an untenable world-order:

> (der profet zu gott)
>
> aber es ist nicht wichtig dass sie nicht sünde tun sondern
> dass sie ausgerotten [sic!] werden . . .
> anstatt dass
> du sie ausrottest
> immer hoffst du . . .

Jetzt ist die Zeit angebrochen, wo Er sie vernichten wird. Er ist gekommen mit seinem Wasser. Ich aber will hinuntergehen in die Städte denn auch ich will untergehen und vernichtet werden, damit nichts mehr bleibe.[33]

The cities of Sodom and Gomorrha, which have been rebuilt and are now "unzerstörbar," are destroyed nevertheless, along with their modern counterparts. The purpose of this universal *memento mori* is made clear by Brecht in a planned preface to *Der Untergang der Paradiesstadt Miami:*

29 BBA 156/34
30 GW 8, p. 262
31 BBA 214
32 BBA 214/18
33 BBA 214/20

Beinahe jeder von uns erinnert sich an den Untergang der römischen Städte Herculaneum, Pompeji und Staböä, der vor nunmehr 2000 Jahren stattgefunden hat. Es ist dies ein Beweis für die Lebenskraft des römischen Volkes, das, sein Unglück dem Ruhm überliefernd, anrufend die Solidarität der Menschheit, das Entsetzen zweier Jahrhunderte [-tausende?] für sich beanspruchte. Weniger auf Ruhm bedacht, die Solidarität der Menschheit verwünschend, am ehesten noch ihrem Entsetzen Bestand wünschend, also aus einem ganz anderen Gefühl heraus [wollen wir] unternehmen, der Erinnerung an den zu unserer Zeit stattgefundenen Untergang der Paradiesstadt Miami einige Dauer zu verleihen. Sind doch seit dem Erdbeben von San Francisco erst wenige Jahre, kaum ein Menschenalter verflossen und schon ist es im Gedächtnis der Menschen zum Triumph der Dummköpfe und zum Schaden der Klügeren beinahe völlig ausgetilgt.[34]

That neither of these projects was completed can no doubt be largely explained by Brecht's decision to collaborate with Weill on the "large scale tragic opera" *Aufstieg und Fall der Stadt Mahagonny*. Much of the *Miami* material was simply taken over (the hurricane, place names, the idea of a "Paradiesstadt"), and the basic plan of presenting an "Untergang" of the order of the Great Flood or the eruption of Vesuvius was transferred to the symbolic "Aufbau" and destruction of a mythical city which, like Sodom or Gomorrha, would incarnate the type of the "Großstadt" for its century. In the process, the original source of the catastrophe — an "act of God" — is replaced by the "acts of men"; Mahagonny falls "on account of the crimes, the licentiousness and the general confusion of its inhabitants." As we shall see, the opera shows this process in its plot; the hurricane spares Mahagonny only in its natural form — it reappears as the basic anarchy of society. Clearly, however, Brecht's intention on beginning to write the text was to produce an apocalypse of the type which he had been planning in *Die Sintflut,* a climax to the negative development of his early work, and the "Weltuntergang" which he describes is not the end of a class or a particular phase of Western society, but of a whole historical period. The tendency to "de-universalise" this crisis is a later attempt at "Zurücknahme" — in 1930, when he revised the opera for publication in the *Versuche,* Brecht, as "frischgebackener Marxist," could no longer allow himself the luxury of such a thorough-going nihilism.

Fortunately, an earlier version of the text is preserved in the piano score of 1929, published by Universal Edition, Vienna.[35] It differs from the later version in a number of important respects. Above all, its hero, Jimmy Mahony (the German names of the *Versuche* version were introduced to make the "local

---

34 BBA 214/23
35 *Aufstieg und Fall der Stadt Mahagonny,* Oper von Kurt Weill, Text von Brecht, Wien 1929

relevance" of the opera clear[36]), remains unrepentant to the end, and exhorts his fellows to continue to observe the "Gesetze der menschlichen Glückseligkeit" which he has discovered, driving home the point with the singing of a further verse of the "Choral," "Gegen Verführung":

> Ich wünsche, daß ihr alle euch durch meinen schrecklichen Tod nicht abhalten laßt, zu leben wie es euch paßt, ohne Sorge. Denn auch ich bereue nicht, daß ich getan habe, was mir beliebt.[37]

This speech is in marked contrast to Paul's farewell in the *Versuche* version:

> Jetzt erkenne ich: als ich diese Stadt betrat, um mir mit Geld Freude zu kaufen, war mein Untergang besiegelt. Jetzt sitze ich hier und habe doch nichts gehabt. Ich war es, der sagte: jeder muß sich ein Stück Fleisch herausschneiden, mit jedem Messer. Da war das Fleisch faul! Die Freude, die ich kaufte, war keine Freude, und die Freiheit für Geld war keine Freiheit. Ich aß und wurde nicht satt, ich trank und wurde durstig. Gebt mir doch ein Glas Wasser![38]

Both Brecht and Weill felt the need of a "clarification of the events in Act 3" as a result of the permière in Leipzig. This "clarification," Weill writes, makes clear "that the final demonstrations are in no wise 'Communistic' — it is simply that Mahagonny, like Sodom and Gomorrha, falls on account of the crimes, the licentiousness and the general confusion of its inhabitants."[39] Even in translation, the similarity of this last phrase to the "title" which Brecht added to Scene 20 in the *Versuche* version is enlightening. It seems probable that the major alterations in the *Versuche* version date from this revision; in particular, as we have seen, Paul's farewell speech is radically changed. Further, his execution is now delayed until after the singing of "Das Spiel von Gott in Mahagonny." In an intermediate version, which was used for the recording of the work, Jim's execution occurs at the beginning of the "Spiel"; the introductory dialogue ("ob es für uns einen Gott gibt") has already been added.[40] It is clear that Brecht and Weill are primarily concerned to tighten the structure here by motivating the insertion of "Gott in Mahagonny" from the action itself. Similarly, Brecht omitted the "Benares Song" from the *Versuche* version as irrelevant to the main strand of the action. The final scene also receives a general "Zuspitzung." The

---

36 cf. piano score, p. 3: "Da die menschlichen Vergnügungen, die für Geld zu haben sind, einander immer und überall aufs Haar gleichen, da die Vergnügungsstadt Mahagony also im weitesten Sinne international ist, können die Namen der Helden in jeweils landesübliche umgeändert werden."
37 op.cit., p. 300
38 GW 2, p. 560—1
39 Drew, op.cit., p. 20
40 Booklet supplied with the recording on Philips L09418—20L, p. 31

song "Aber dieses ganze Mahagonny," which in the first version had been merely repeated, here is altered accordingly to correspond to Paul's new insight into the vanity of "die Freiheit für Geld":

> Nämlich dieses schöne Mahagonny
> Hat alles, solange ihr Geld habt.
> Dann gibt es alles
> Weil alles käuflich ist
> Und weil es nichts gibt, was man nicht kaufen kann.[41]

Like the original song, this version appears also in its negative form later in the scene:

> Aber dieses ganze Mahagonny
> Hat nichts für euch, wenn ihr kein Geld habt
> Für Geld gibt's alles
> Und ohne Geld nichts
> Drum ist's das Geld nur, woran man sich halten kann.[42]

The "Tafeln" carried by the processions are supplemented by a number of new "Inschriften," which also stress the rejection of Mahagonny:

> FÜR DIE TEUERUNG
> FÜR DEN KAMPF ALLER GEGEN ALLE
> FÜR DEN CHAOTISCHEN ZUSTAND UNSERER STÄDTE
> FÜR DAS EIGENTUM
> FÜR DIE ENTEIGNUNG DER ANDEREN
> FÜR DIE LIEBE
> FÜR DIE KÄUFLICHKEIT DER LIEBE
> FÜR DIE NATÜRLICHE UNORDNUNG DER DINGE
> FÜR DIE TAPFERKEIT GEGEN DIE WEHRLOSEN
> FÜR DIE EHRE DER MÖRDER
> FÜR DIE GRÖSSE DES SCHMUTZES
> FÜR DIE UNSTERBLICHKEIT DER GEMEINHEIT[43]

Characteristically, two of the undialectic opposites of the first version are now omitted, as belonging to the world of "der neue Mensch":

> FÜR DIE NATÜRLICHE ORDNUNG DER DINGE
> FÜR DIE FREIHEIT ALLER LEUTE[44]

---

41 GW 2, p. 561—2
42 GW 2, p. 563
43 GW 2, p. 561—2
44 Piano score, p. 325

It is clear, then, that the "Ausgang" of *Mahagonny* in May 1930 is different from that of the original plan which, we may assume, the piano score of 1929 follows reasonably closely. The *Versuche* version represents an adaptation by Brecht of a text from which he had already distanced himself to a considerable extent, an adaptation made when work on the first "Lehrstücke" had already begun. And yet Weill writes in his letter that the demonstrations at the end are "in no way Communistic," a conclusion which seems to be borne out by the form of Brecht's alterations. The important change between the two versions is not the provision of a "way out," Communistic or not, but the attaining by Paul of the insight that "das Fleisch war faul," the replacement of Jim's earlier "Einverständnis" with his own execution and his exhortation to the others to continue to observe the "laws" he has discovered by a rejection of Mahagonny and all that it stands for. There is, then, a vital difference between the two: in the first, Brecht's sympathy with Jim is obvious, like Jim he accepts the death and destruction of the end of the opera with a cynical resignation which, as we have seen, is typical of the early work; in the second, he leads Paul to the insight that he has himself reached, that ". . . die Freiheit für Geld war keine Freiheit," that the anarchism of *Mahagonny* is a worthless delusion. When we speak, then, of *Mahagonny,* we must be conscious of the fact that with this work Brecht undertook a process of "Umfunktionieren" quite as radical as with other of his plays, and that *Mahagonny* is not really one work, but two. To speak of the opera as an "allegory of the end of capitalism" is to identify oneself with the tendency of the later version to some extent, but it brings one into conflict with the earlier, and with those features of it which persist in the later version. Brecht cannot be "distanced" from *Mahagonny* quite so easily; even in 1930 he is unable to provide Paul with an alternative, or even the hope of one, and it is difficult to deny either his involvement in the severe nihilism of the earlier *Mahagonny* or its organic relationship to the world of the early works. As we have seen, both *Mahagonny* and *Die Dreigroschenoper* were, in a sense, later "zurückgenommen" by Brecht; in 1930 he was no longer prepared to take up the position from which they had originally been written, and attempted to transfer this new "distance" into the works themselves, both by actual alterations and by new production methods. The full significance of *Mahagonny* becomes plain only when we are able to see it as a logical and necessary development of the early work, and to assess Brecht's attitude to it in 1930 in much the same way as we might, for example, analyse Goethe's later treatment of the material in *Urfaust* as against his original conception. Brecht's "Auseinandersetzung" with *Mahagonny* reflects his changing attitude to his early work as a whole; in this process, *Mahagonny,* by virtue of its exemplary and representative character, comes to stand for the entire period.

As we have seen, the word "Mahagonny" was first used by Brecht in connection with the Nazi demonstrations in München in the early twenties. By

1930, its meaning has expanded considerably; as Adorno writes, "die Stadt Mahagonny ist eine Darstellung der sozialen Welt, in der wir leben."[45] "Mahagonny" comes to stand for the world of the big cities after the First World War; H. H. Stuckenschmidt even claims that "the atmosphere of Berlin in the twenties has found no more anguished expression than in this opera . . ."[46] The "zynisch-dummer Stammtisch-Staat" of 1923 persists in *Mahagonny,* but as only one of the levels of significance; the city becomes an allegory for a whole way of life.

III

> "Alle wahrhaft Suchenden werden
> enttäuscht."
> Title to Scene 8, *Aufstieg und*
> *Fall der Stadt Mahagonny*

In a review of Giorgio Strehler's production of *Mahagonny* at the Piccolo Scala in Milan in 1964, Siegfried Melchinger[47] writes of the opera as a "Mysterienspiel," a mystery play in the sense of Hofmannsthal's *Jedermann,* which Reinhardt had made so famous in his Salzburg production. *Jedermann,* following closely the English mediaeval morality *Everyman,* has the mystery of death and the reckoning which comes after as its theme; in it, Hofmannsthal tries to re-create the simplicity, the naivety of the mediaeval world-picture. For him, the "mystery-play" is a simplification, a retreat from the complexities of modern life to the "eternal verities." *Mahagonny* stands in the same relation to *Jedermann* as the *Hauspostille* ("Des Teufels Gebetbuch"[48]) to more conventional prayer-books. It is a "taking-back," a "Zurücknahme" of the Christian mystery. For the men of Mahagonny there is no "Jenseits," no hell even but that on earth; God has become an irrelevance to the world of human suffering. When he does appear in Act 3, it is as a slightly senile bourgeois papa reproving his unruly children for their behaviour in a world with which he has lost touch, like the God of the early "Hymne an Gott":

> Ließest die Armen arm sein manches Jahr
> Weil ihre Sehnsucht schöner als dein Himmel war

---

45 T. W. Adorno, "Mahagonny," reprinted in *Moments Musicaux,* Frankfurt 1964, p. 131
46 In an essay written for the booklet accompanying the recording, "Mahagonny — City of Nets," p. 13
47 "Mahagonny als Mysterienspiel," *Theater Heute,* Mai 1964, pp. 32ff.
48 cf. Karl Thieme, "Des Teufels Gebetbuch? Eine Auseinandersetzung mit dem Werk Bertolt Brechts," *Hochland,* XXIX (1932), No. 5

Starben sie leider, bevor mit dem Lichte du kamst
Starben sie selig doch — und verfaulten sofort.[49]

In the early poems God is irrelevant, unnecessary; he is unable to equal the magnitude of human joy and suffering for which he is theoretically responsible, and arrives too late to do anyone any good, becoming a mere figure of fun. One imagines that a good deal of Brecht's aggression towards his father's generation is drawn on for these characterisations. Unlike Kafka, he revolted from the first with great self-assurance; "Die Leute meiner Klasse gefielen mir nicht."[50] He was determined to find a way which was not theirs. The bourgeois Christian deity became for him a symbol of this "disconnection," the attempt of the bourgeoisie to impose its out-dated code on a world which had grown beyond it.

Mahagonny deals in a schematic way with the failure of one "wahrhaft Suchender," Bert Brecht, to find any other way, any solution to the problem. It reveals the complete bankruptcy of Brecht's "Utopian" thought at this stage; a moderately acceptable heaven is available neither on earth nor in the hereafter. The mystery play is thus turned "upside down" and becomes a demonstration of the impossibility of salvation. The "Enttäuschung der wahrhaft Suchenden" is carried out with a thoroughness reminiscent of Jedermann's judgement after his death, and with a similar "ritualistic" approach, but no "act of kindness" can redeem Jimmy/Paul; he is left facing the "Nichts" which he himself has summoned up. There is even a "Choral" to point the moral of the "play," which contains the essence of Jim's insight and can almost be regarded as the "text" which the whole work illustrates:

Laßt euch nicht verführen
Es gibt keine Wiederkehr.
Der Tag steht vor den Türen
Ihr könnt schon Nachtwind spüren
Es kommt kein Morgen mehr.

Laßt euch nicht betrügen
Das Leben wenig ist.
Schlürft es in vollen Zügen
Es kann euch nicht genügen
Wenn ihr es lassen müßt.

Laßt euch nicht vertrösten
Ihr habt nicht zu viel Zeit.
Laßt Moder den Verwesten
Das Leben ist am größten
Es steht nicht mehr bereit.

49 GW 8, p. 54
50 cf. GW 9, p. 721, "Verjagt mit gutem Grund"

Laßt euch nicht verführen
Zu Fron und Ausgezehr.
Was kann euch Angst noch rühren
Ihr sterbt mit allen Tieren
Und es kommt nichts nachher.[51]

Already in the first stanza the essential situation of *Mahagonny* is set out: "Der Tag steht vor den Türen / Ihr könnt schon Nachtwind spüren / Es kommt kein Morgen mehr." What remains is only the brief space of day before night and "Nichts." The imminence of the end is superbly conveyed in the image of day "standing before the doorways," ready for the "Aufbruch," impatient to go its way. Brecht meets the inevitable approach of the "Nichts" with an anarchistic exhortation to "enjoy": "Schlürft es in vollen Zügen," already a prefiguration of Paul's discovery of "die Gesetze der menschlichen Glückseligkeit." Virtue has no reward in Mahagonny; in a criminal society "Entsagen" becomes a crime, a crime against one's right to enjoy the little of "day" that is left. But the "Genuß" itself is overshadowed by the approaching destruction: "Das Leben ist am größten / Es steht nicht mehr bereit." As in *Im Dickicht der Städte,* "das Chaos ist aufgebraucht," the expansion of *Baal* is no longer possible. The last stanza turns to a type of "social criticism" common in the early poetry: it demonstrates the untenability of "society" out of a feeling of pity for the injured "animal" caught in its trap. The "victims" to whom Brecht addresses himself have "nothing to lose." The poem "Von der Kindesmörderin Marie Farrar" is typical of this approach: Marie Farrar's damaged personality is held up for us to inspect critically and to pass judgement on, but there is not a trace of the ill-disguised pathos of Benn's early poems; sympathy is only apparent in the naturalistic carefulness of the detail, in the author's determination to present the experience in its own terms. Brecht's "leidende Kreaturen" are described with the same neutrality as Büchner's, a neutrality which springs from a complete moral identification with suffering humanity and a determination to see life "as it really is," unaltered by the pathos of idealism. *Mahagonny,* too, attacks a "Modell" of contemporary society with great savagery, but without the pathos that belongs to the revolutionary; its principle is rather the recognition of the full tragic banality of this existence and its "Ausweglosigkeit." All in all, the "Choral" is like a programme for the attempts of the four "heroes," Paul, Jakob, Heinrich and Joe, to find in *Mahagonny* the goal of their search for "das Land, wo es besser zu leben ist," and their fore-doomed failure in this quest.

The elements of "Fron und Ausgezehr" are obvious behind the facade of the "Stadt des Vergnügens" that Begbick, Willy and Moses set up at the beginning of

---

51 GW 2, p. 527–8. Cf. Walter Benjamin, *Versuche über Brecht,* Frankfurt 1966, pp. 56ff.

the opera, as shown only too clearly in Begbick's "translation" of its name, "Netzestadt":

> Sie soll sein wie ein Netz
> Das für die eßbaren Vögel gestellt wird.[52]

Although the founders of Mahagonny are scarcely "dämonisch," it is important to realise that Mahagonny is their last hope too; they themselves have no way out, they can go no further, and yet cannot return. The "end-situation" of *Mahagonny* applies as much to them as to their "victims." Begbick herself has changed greatly since *Mann ist Mann;* her fight for survival has lost much of the incidental humour and humanity which adorned it in India. Mahagonny is her "letzter großer Plan" — like her quarry, Paul, she sees the end close at hand. The rebellious "Aber etwas fehlt" with which Paul rejects not only Mahagonny but a whole way of life is raised to a higher degree in Begbick's struggle to stay alive by making money out of a "Spaß" which she sells to others but is no longer able to accept herself. She sees the "bankruptcy" of this "Spaß" as clearly as Paul; they share an anger that things are as they are, a perpetual dissatisfaction. Both pursue their fate with a curiously aggressive desire for the catastrophe, a sensation that the end can be no worse than the present in their eyes. Like Mutter Courage, Begbick has thrown her "emotional luggage" overboard in order to stay afloat:

> Alle wollen etwas haben von mir, und ich habe nichts mehr. Was soll ich ihnen geben, daß sie hierbleiben und mich leben lassen? [53]

She is Jenny grown older; there is a striking similarity in emotional tone between her confession:

> Auch ich bin einmal an einer Mauer gestanden
> Mit einem Mann
> Und wir haben Worte getauscht
> Und von der Liebe gesprochen.
> Aber das Geld ist hin
> Und mit ihm auch die Sinnlichkeit.[54]

and Jenny's song in Scene 16,

> Ja, Liebe, das ist leicht gesagt:
> Doch, solang man täglich älter wird

52 GW 2, p. 502
53 GW 2, p. 515
54 loc.cit.

Da wird nicht nach Liebe gefragt
Da muß man seine kurze Zeit benützen.[55]

Jenny's refusal to come to Paul's aid in Act 3 ("Lächerlich! Was wir Mädchen alles sollen!") shows her closeness not only to Begbick, but also to Paul; she supports her action with his own song, "Denn wie man sich bettet, so liegt man ..." She is after all only following his newly-discovered "laws of human happiness": "Wenn das Dach aber durchbricht, geh weg!" The difference then between Paul, Jenny and Begbick is not one of kind, but of degree, and Begbick is perhaps the closest to the "brink" in her Garga-like attempts to survive "mit dem nackten Leben in der Tasche." She has gone farther towards attaining her "kleinste Größe" than the others. Paul's downfall, like Eilif's and Schweizerkas', results from his failure to achieve this "kleinste Größe"; he exposes himself by his "Tugend," his loyalty to Joe, which contradicts his own law. Begbick becomes the symbol of this law, which takes its revenge on Paul for his failure to discard the irrelevance of "feelings." She is something of an evil angel of justice, a wall of harsh consequence against which Paul is shattered. He has not learnt the lesson Brecht had taught Galy Gay with such thoroughness in *Mann ist Mann*, that "personality" is irrelevant. The concept of "loyalty" seems from the first to be bound up with autobiographical elements in the opera. The four wood-cutters who appear from the black forests of Alaska in Scene 3, ready to try the pleasures of Mahagonny, are strongly reminiscent of a group of young men setting out from Augsburg to experience the "Großstadtleben" of München and Berlin in the twenties. One is struck by the similarity between Münsterer's account of the "Brechtkreis" in Augsburg[56] and its gradual breaking up over the years and the overall scheme of *Mahagonny*. The kind of cheerful jargon the four indulge in is closely paralleled by the good-natured banter of many of Brecht's more conversational poems of the Augsburg period; even for the nicknames and the characeristic relation of Paul to the others as "primus inter pares" it is easy to find precedents in the Augsburg Brecht. We shall see, too, that this "group of four," with one "rebel" or "dissident" recurs constantly in Brecht's work in these years, and that the development in his work is mirrored in the relationship of the "one" to the "group." Paul, like the B. B. of the early poems, is always the first to protest, to rebel; it is hard to ignore in Scene 8 an element of bitterness on Brecht's part at the ease with which his companions had accommodated themselves to the "Ruhe und Eintracht" of the conformist "Spießers Utopia." In the final scenes there seems to be an increasingly elegiac realisation of his own isolation from the easy camaraderie of the Augsburg days.

The formula "Ruhe und Eintracht" becomes, in fact, a kind of pivot around which the play is constructed, the central paradox on which Mahagonny

---

55 GW 2, p. 546
56 H. O. Münsterer, *Bert Brecht — Erinnerungen aus den Jahren 1917—22*, Zurich 1963

is built. In Scene 1 Willy and Moses present their new "city" as an answer to the
general longing for a "Land, wo es besser zu leben ist":

> Aber dieses ganze Mahagonny
> Ist nur, weil alles so schlecht ist
> Weil keine Ruhe herrscht
> Und keine Eintracht
> Und weil es nichts gibt
> Woran man sich halten kann.[57]

But in Scene 9 Paul sees the cause of Mahagonny's failure to be this "paradise"
precisely in its "Ruhe und Eintracht":

> Ach, mit eurem ganzen Mahagonny
> Wird nie ein Mensch glücklich werden
> Weil zu viel Ruhe herrscht
> Und zu viel Eintracht
> Und weil's zu viel gibt
> Woran man sich halten kann.[58]

The "Ruhe und Eintracht" of Mahagonny is "faul," like the "Fleisch" of Paul's
farewell speech, because it conceals a basic "dialectic of anarchy" inherent in the
structure of this "paradise," a dialectic which Paul uncovers and brings to the
surface.[59] "Die Ruhe und die Eintracht für Geld" is thus "keine Ruhe und keine
Eintracht." It is the conservative superstructure with which "Gewalt" tries to
disguise itself as "Ordnung." Paul's realisation of this basic anarchy in a very real
sense "causes" the typhoon, which is only a manifestation of "die Gewalt als
Grund der gegenwärtigen Ordnung" (Adorno). As "wahrhaft Suchender" he sees
the falsity of Mahagonny's "Ruhe und Eintracht," its failure to be anything
more than a parody of the "original unity," manipulated by its owners for their
own ends. "Etwas fehlt."

From the beginning, Begbick is conscious of this "dialectic." Mahagonny is
both "Netz für die eßbaren Vögel" and "earthly paradise:"

> Überall gibt es Mühe und Arbeit
> Aber hier gibt es Spaß.
> Denn es ist die Wollust der Männer
> Nicht zu leiden und alles zu dürfen . . .
> Und die großen Taifune kommen nicht bis hierher.[60]

---

[57] GW 2, p. 503
[58] GW 2, p. 523
[59] cf. Adorno, op.cit.
[60] GW 2, p. 502

"Spaß," "Nicht zu leiden und alles zu dürfen" is the bait with which she proposes to attract the "birds," but it is a "Spaß" which is calculated to bring about their eventual capture and destruction. The "Taifun" which finds its way to Mahagonny despite the prediction is only a symbol for Paul's "Entlarvung" of her strategy. So long as Begbick is able to keep the dialectic of anarchy under control, by disguising it with a cloak of "Ordnung," of "Ruhe und Eintracht," her city is safe. But when it becomes the acknowledged law of Mahagonny, it overpowers her with the others. Her first reaction to Paul's discovery sees in it only a possible business alternative: "Du meinst also, es war falsch, daß ich etwas verboten habe? !"[61] Paul is prepared to pay for his anarchy. She seems to be unaware of the force of the hurricane which has been unleashed; the "Gewalt" which Paul has summoned up brings about the downfall of all by showing the falseness of the whole system. "Alles zu dürfen" includes for Begbick a series of prohibitions which she imposes on her city, which ensure that her profit will not be endangered, that the present order will not be upset; Paul's "Du darfst es!" is a radical attack on the system itself. Like Baal, he recognises the "asocial" character of his society, Mahagonny, and invents a new code of "asocial" behaviour to match it, though Paul's revolt is now based on a deep insight into the workings of the capitalism of the "Großstädte." He has attained, to repeat Adorno's phrase, "die [Erkenntnis] von Gewalt als dem Grunde der gegenwärtigen Ordnung und von der Zweideutigkeit, in der Ordnung und Gewalt gegeneinanderstehen." It is in this "paradoxes Zugleich" that Adorno sees the seeds of Mahagonny's destruction:

> weil es nichts gibt, woran man sich halten kann, weil blinde Natur herrscht, darum gibt es zuviel, woran man sich halten kann, Recht und Sitte; sie sind des gleichen Ursprungs; darum muß Mahagonny untergehen.[62]

The hurricane spares Mahagonny only temporarily; the meeting of the anarchy of nature and the anarchy of society in "Angst vor dem Tode" shows the dialectic itself as a "Naturzwang" which brings about the eventual collapse of the "Netzestadt." Paul's "fall from high estate" is a rather Samson-like effort; it demonstrates the fundamental impossibility of what we might call "communal anarchy."

The destruction of Mahagonny is at the same time the destruction of a whole possibility of life for Brecht; the "Spaß" which Begbick offers the men of Mahagonny is closely related to the idea of "Spaß" which recurs so frequently in the early theoretical writings, full of overtones of Brecht's earlier enthusiasm for America, for sport, for the "modern." This world is destroyed by Paul's "Drang zur Selbstvernichtung," his determination to pull the "asocial," anarchical

61 GW 2, p. 529
62 Adorno, op.cit., p. 133

society around him down about his ears, rather than endure its perpetual assault on his vision of an original unity. Paul's "Gesetze der menschlichen Glückseligkeit" are not the laws of a new Utopia, they are designed for the stage of history where "Der Tag steht vor den Türen"; he is quite aware of their destructive tendency: "Denn gerade so ist der Mensch: / Er muß zerstören, was da ist." Like the heroes of the early poems, Paul sees an essential equivalence between a destructive, impersonal nature (here in the form of the hurricane) and a blind anarchy at the root of society. In both, "blinde Natur herrscht." In his impatience for the end, Paul summons this "blinde Natur" to the fore:

> Wir brauchen keinen Hurrikan
> Wir brauchen keinen Taifun
> Denn was er an Schrecken tun kann
> Das können wir selber tun.[63]

It is at this stage that the hurricane becomes "unnecessary"; it is replaced by the social anarchy Paul has instituted. In this sense we can hardly say that its very Baden-Baden-like "removal" from the opera "entreißt die historische Dialektik dem Naturzwang";[64] it is rather than the "Naturzwang" persists as "die historische Dialektik," the same content in a different form.

It would seem, then, that the society which Brecht destroys in *Mahagonny* stands as a symbol for the whole world which surrounds him, that here the "Selbstvernichtungsprozeß" of the early work reaches its eventual conclusion in a destruction of self and world. *Mahagonny* is not "historisiert," it stands as an allegory of "die gegenwärtige Ordnung," to which no alternative is advanced, in the same way that Brecht, in "Vom armen B. B," had written: "Und nach uns wird kommen: nichts Nennenswertes." Both Adorno and Schuhmacher,[65] however, see in this destruction of the present order an implicit commitment on Brecht's part to a "new order," which is to arise out of the ruins of Mahagonny. Schuhmacher tacitly assumes that the work represents an "apocalypse of capitalism" written from a Marxist point of view, and criticises it for its quite understandable failure to justify such an interpretation; Adorno's analysis is so similar to Brecht's later expressed attitudes that it seems likely that this perceptive and forward-looking essay itself had considerable influence on his later development. He equates Mahagonny with "die gegenwärtige Ordnung," which he sees by definition as "capitalistic": "Es gibt in Wahrheit, zumindest fürs deutsche Bewußtsein, keinen unkapitalistischen Raum."[66] The fall of capitalism which he sees in *Mahagonny* — "die Darstellung seines Unterganges an

---

63 GW 2, p. 527
64 Adorno, op.cit., p. 134
65 Ernst Schuhmacher, *Die dramatischen Versuche Bertolt-Brechts 1918—1933*, Berlin 1955, pp. 262ff.
66 Adorno, op.cit., p. 131

der Dialektik der Anarchie, die ihm innewohnt" — is thus free of the separative
sense in which Schuhmacher uses this phrase, as representing only "part" of
society, which is to deny the very strong sense of "Weltuntergang" which
permeates the opera and to give Brecht a detachment from his work which does
not seem to be justified by the work itself. Yet, for Adorno, "Die Stadt
Mahagonny ist eine Darstellung der sozialen Welt, in der wir leben, entworfen
aus der Vogelperspektive *einer real befreiten Gesellschaft.*" This "real befreite
Gesellschaft" is in fact, socialism: "So ist in Mahagonny die bürgerliche Welt
enthüllt als absurd, gemessen an einer sozialistischen, die sich verschweigt." The
"new order" "verschweigt sich," it is omitted from the work itself but is both
starting-point and proper criterion for the work, to be supplied by the reader.
Although "keine klassenlose Gesellschaft [wird] als positives Maß des ver-
worfenen gegenwärtigen sichtbar," it can be "deduced" from the work. This
seems to stand in some opposition to the statement that, for the German
consciousness, there is in fact "kein unkapitalistischer Raum"; it requires some
further qualification, i.e., that it is the necessity or the desirability of socialism
which can be "deduced" from *Mahagonny,* rather than socialism itself. This
supplied argument seems in fact to express Adorno's conclusions, but it also
makes clear the extent to which his own argument is "supplied." If the evidence
"verschweigt sich," we can hardly reach a definite judgement without a direct
statement by Brecht of such an intention, and even then, the procedure of
applying the author's intention to a work which does not in any real sense
"contain" it seems very questionable. Of course, such a statement by Brecht is
lacking, and we have seen precisely the difficulties involved in applying later
statements to a work which was virtually complete before the change to
Marxism; it would seem, rather, that a study of the early work tends to support
the view that the "real befreite Gesellschaft" which "verschweigt sich" in
Mahagonny is, in fact, held by Brecht to be an impossibility, that the destruction
of Mahagonny is an allegory of a total apocalyptic "Weltuntergang" envisaged by
Brecht at this stage, the furthest development of the pessimism and nihilism of
his early period. We must distinguish between a belief in the "desirability" of a
"real befreite Gesellschaft" and a conviction of its *feasibility.* We might deduce
from *Mahagonny* the author's disgust with the world of the present (although
even here, as we have seen, there is a curious ambivalence, a delight in
destruction), but to claim that it "implies" a new society is scarcely justifiable.
Nor does Brecht's "disgust" seem to be of this world-changing kind. The first
version clearly demonstrates Paul's "Einverständnis" with his fate and his
affirmation of the whole development, and even in the *Versuche* version, though
the rejection of Mahagonny has been made clear, we are presented with no
alternative, indeed, the final scene becomes even more universal in its pessimism
because an element of the "tragic" has been added. Paul's insight is not of a
forward-looking kind; it comes too late to provide anything more than a

"Steigerung" of the final conflagration. In its own terms, *Mahagonny* seems to reject any hope of a new society, it is a kind of anti-Utopia, a Utopia *ad absurdum*, designed to prove the impossibility of "das Land, wo es besser zu leben ist." Paul, like Kafka's "Hungerkünstler," is doomed never to become "satt," because "die Speise, die ihm schmeckt" does not exist; unlike him, he wishes to starve the rest of the world as well.

Nevertheless, Adorno's essay remains of central importance, for its analysis of what it terms the "verschobene Optik" of *Mahagonny,* and for its anticipation of the major problem of the later works — the relationship between intention and execution, between the work itself and the author's statements about its "direction." In strikingly similar terms to those of the later Brecht, he writes:

> Die Projektion durchs Medium des kindlichen Auges verändert die Wirklichkeit so weit, bis ihr Grund verständlich wird; verflüchtigt sie jedoch nicht zur Metapher, sondern faßt sie zugleich in ihrer unvermittelten geschichtlichen Konkretion.[67]

He sees the "schräge, infantile Betrachtung" of *Mahagonny* as an "Entzauberung der kapitalistischen Ordnung":

> Alles ist in eine regelhaft verschobene Optik gebracht, welche die Oberflächengestalt des bürgerlichen Lebens verzerrt zur Grimasse einer Wirklichkeit, die Ideologien sonst verdecken.

The path from "Entzauberung" to "Verfremdung" is not difficult to follow. The false "Optik" of a society which has become alienated from itself is neutralised by a second, "verschobene Optik" which reveals its true basis; the two technically false perspectives together achieve a representation of the "true" reality, which is concealed by the ideological superstructure. Society is presented from the point of view of "das [ihr] immanente Märchen," the apparent grotesquerie is designed to penetrate the mass of "entfremdete Perspektiven." This "schräge, infantile Betrachtung" can be seen in its origins in the work of the very early Brecht. In "Apfelböck oder Die Lilie auf dem Felde"[68] the perspective is consciously limited to that of the child-murderer himself, and this limitation, this "gespielte Naivität" is typical of the early poems. It is indeed, as Adorno puts it, "eine Vogelperspektive," but can perhaps be understood best as an attempt to see the world from a "pre-conscious" point of view, to enter into the anarchical and unconscious state of nature. The "natural" for Brecht is free from any "direction," it is a rejection of consciousness. It is only in the later works that the "Vogelperspektive" becomes a conscious "device"; here, it is

---

67   op.cit., p. 132
68   GW 8, p. 173

independent and self-justifying, and seems to be an almost instinctive, automatic procedure on Brecht's part.

In his later theories, Brecht tends to take up a position very similar to that of Adorno, and it is no coincidence that the real "beginning" of these theories is to be found in the "Anmerkungen" Brecht wrote for the publication of Mahagonny in the Versuche.[69] The rejection of Mahagonny which is conveyed in Paul's new farewell speech is, if anything, more extreme in the notes. It is clear that Brecht has distanced himself from the work a great deal; not surprisingly, the new concepts he uses seem often more appropriate to the early "Lehrstücke" which were in the process of composition. The "possibility" which is not present in Mahagonny, the "Ausweg," is now a basic conviction:

> Wirklicher Fortschritt hat als Ursache die Unhaltbarkeit eines wirklichen Zustandes und als Folge seine Veränderung.[70]

These words, referring to the problem of a new "opera," can in fact be taken in a much wider sense; they mark the emergence of a new kind of reasoning in Brecht, which dominates the later period. Mahagonny demonstrates with rare thoroughness "die Unhaltbarkeit eines wirklichen Zustandes," that of the contemporary world itself; the conclusion to be drawn from this "Unhaltbarkeit" is now "Veränderung." This is in effect Adorno's argument, but we must stress once more that it remains extraneous to the opera. The same writer who in "Der Nachgeborene" had directly denied the possibility of an "Ausweg" is now able to see "wirklicher Fortschritt" in "change."

In this book, I wish to avoid at all costs the facile and quite inadequate interpretation of the later Brecht which depreciates the seriousness of his theories "in favour of" his works and supposes some kind of saving intellectual dishonesty which came into play the moment he indulged in "creative" writing. It is, perhaps, the absence of this kind of intellectual dishonesty which makes Brecht's solution possible and fruitful. On the other hand, a critical approach which itself attempts to demonstrate a dialectic process in Brecht's development cannot afford to dismiss the "antithetical" position of Brecht's early work without risking a total misunderstanding; nor is it realistic to assume that this "antithesis" leaves no trace in the later work. We have seen that the "perspective" of the early work is a "natural" one and that it grows out of a unified and organic "Weltbild"; to replace this consciously, to turn the "Perspektive des kindlichen Auges" into a Marxist "Verfremdungstechnik" is clearly going to require more than a simple decision on Brecht's part. The artistic method of the early plays, which rely almost entirely for their unity on the

---

69 GW 17, pp. 1004ff.
70 p. 1015n.

unity of the "vision" on which they are based and reject any conscious "aesthetic" procedure as irrelevant, does not lend itself easily to the highly conscious analysis of the Marxist plays, which reject "instinct" as largely illusory and stand in a very complex relationship indeed to "nature." It is, then, not surprising that the opposition between the "Lehrstücke" of the thirties and the early plays is extreme, and that a "synthesis" of these two possibilities seems to be achieved only in the last plays. If this is so, then an analysis of these plays should be able to demonstrate the "survival" in them of the antithetical position of the early work, but at a higher level. We must avoid the fashionable views that here Brecht wrote "good" plays because he was a "bad" Marxist or that he wrote "bad" plays because he was a "good" Marxist; the problem is rather to estimate the degree of success he had in combining, in these later works, his own rather individual brand of Marxism with the demands of his "literary method," which we shall see to be the main form in which the "difficulties" of the earlier period persist. It is outside the scope of the present work to discuss whether this problem is in fact inherent in a literature which calls itself Marxist; we must concern ourselves rather with an analysis of this particular attempt. An understanding of Brecht's personal Marxism is, of course, vital for an understanding of his work, but we should bear in mind that it is not, by itself, enough; the plays and poems have other obligations than merely to say "what Brecht thinks," and conclusions drawn from the handling of a particular scene may tell us more about his literary method than about his political philosophy.

The absence of a "real befreite Gesellschaft," "das Sich-Verschweigen einer sozialistischen Ordnung, an der die gegenwärtige gemessen wird," remains typical of the later works. Between them and *Mahagonny* there is, however, a radical difference. We may be obliged later to see this "Sich-Verschweigen" as an expression of Brecht's inability to present such a society in his work, but at the very least, the later work seems to express the "desirability" of a "true" socialist society. Even if Brecht seldom commits himself to a direct statement as to whether this rationalised "Land, wo es besser zu leben ist" is truly realisable or merely a direction in which we should strive, the direction itself is clear. In *Mahagonny* there is no such direction; the work is written rather from the "perspective" of the "Nichts," which we have seen to dominate the poetry which surrounds its composition, the "Vogelperspektive" of the end of time which does not come, as in the "Sonett über schlechtes Leben." The "Vernichtungsprozeß" achieves full consciousness; the self has set up, "thrown out" an end beyond itself, and now attempts to force itself and the society about it towards this point, which is their total destruction. The individual consciousness demands the destruction of all consciousness. This problem of "overtaking" a fixed but unattainable end-point results in the apparent contradiction of "Wie langsam mir die kurze Zeit verrinnt," the characteristic boredom of a closed development which cannot be brought to its conclusion.

In many ways, this perspective is related to the more typically expressionist tendencies in the early Brecht, his fondness for the dead and the inanimate, the "Wasserleichen" with which his early poetry abounds (*Baal*, "Vom ertrunkenen Mädchen"), which marks even the political satire of the "Legende vom toten Soldaten." Kragler, too, is a "Wasserleiche" returned to life:

> Jetzt bin ich kein Gespenst mehr. Siehst du mein Gesicht wieder? Ist es wie eine Krokodilhaut? Ich sehe schlecht heraus. Ich bin im salzigen Wasser gewesen.[71]

Death becomes for Brecht a mirror which distorts life back to its true shape. "Das Nichts" haunts the early work with something of the bogey-man quality of death to a child, a grotesque consciousness of the interdependence of life and its negation, but it is not until *Mahagonny* that the negation becomes so strong that it inhibits the possibility of any further movement; the stasis of the eye of the hurricane has been reached.

It is perhaps in the clownery of the "Benares Song"[72] that this stasis achieves its most direct expression. Its "Where shall we go?" anticipates oddly the "Wohin soll ich denn gehen?" of later years in East Berlin. The quest for "das Land, wo es besser zu leben ist" with its "blühende Zitronen" and its "luxe, calme et volupté" ends here among the fragments of a ruined language, which like Beckett's in *En attendant Godot* bears the marks of a modern "descent into hell," where the imaginary Utopias of the nineteenth century are no longer accessible. The escapism of art is rejected in the "Benares Song" in a language which is itself consciously anti-artistic (even the "mistakes" in Brecht's English seem to contribute to this effect):

> Worst of all, Benares is said to have been perished by an earthquake: Where shall we go?[73]

It is peculiarly appropriate that the total disillusionment with this perpetual "escape" should express itself in a diction of such nakedness and banality. For the younger Brecht, as for Ionesco, the tragic is intensely banal, it expresses itself in the cliché-ridden language of conversation courses and foreign language "methods."

The later omission of the "Benares Song" was clearly intended to "tighten up" the structure of Act 3, but to regard it merely as an interpolation is to ignore its real function. Coming as it does before the trial and sentence of Jim, it suddenly opens the perspective of the opera in much the same way as those

---

71 GW 1, p. 89. Cf. Bernhard Blume, "Motive der frühen Lyrik Brechts," *Monatshefte*, LVII (1965), pp. 97ff. and 273ff.
72 Now in GW 8, p. 247–8. Brecht later "corrected" the English of the original version.
73 Piano score, p. 293

Act 5 scenes of which Shakespeare is so fond, where apparently unrelated matter is introduced just before the dénouement. The relevance of the action is extended to a universal search for Utopia; the "stellvertretend" quality of Mahagonny is once again impressed on us before the particular action takes its particular end. To remove it is to remove one of the central expressions of the original idea of the opera. Furthermore, the "Benares Song" seems to represent the highest common factor between Brecht and Weill at this stage, a position from which they both retreated later: a total despair with their society and its art and an ability to express it in a form stripped radically of all the politenesses of the salon. Weill's excursions into the fractional world of jazz and the popular song, the "poisonously iridescent" sounds of this music for the end of time, mark the end of a whole movement in Western music. The "universalism" of Mahler and Berg finds its *reductio ad absurdum,* its end-development in Weill, whose music finds its way back to the "people," to the greater audience, not as the beginning of a forward-looking popular revolution in art, as many still thought at the time of the *Dreigroschenoper,* [74] but as the final summing-up of a catastrophe in art and society. The synthesis that Weill achieves is not the thesis of a new triad, it has an "end" quality about it, a "Konsequenz" which matches the pessimism of Brecht's text. It is hard to think of a work after *Mahagonny* which has even been able to approach a comparable synthesis. It is significant that as soon as Weill broke with Brecht his music lost this "Konsequenz" completely and sank back into the world of "Spießers Utopia," of the musical and the operetta. Here it achieves, like Brecht's own peculiar "universal language" of pidgin English,[75] a rare universality by its capacity to combine the most disparate elements into a meaningful theatrical experience. Its texture matches Brecht's diction in its sparseness and nakedness. *Mahagonny* is to a very high degree the "product" of score and libretto rather than merely the "sum," like so many other operas. It depends for its effect on the contrast and interplay of text and music, of stage action and orchestral commentary, and many passages in the text justify themselves fully only in the theatre.

In the analysis of the two most important "scene-complexes" of *Mahagonny* which follows I have attempted to interpret it in this light, as a "work of theatre" which is also a "play of the end of time." Music criticism has a language of its own, and it is doing Weill and Brecht a disservice to attempt to put together what they went to such lengths to keep apart. Nevertheless, although we may be on difficult ground, it is necessary to treat these two complementary factors in performance in a general way from the very point of view where they come together — that of the theatre. *Mahagonny* is a "Gesamtkunstwerk" in a very different sense from Wagner's music dramas; the various "arts" remain

74   cf. Adorno, "Zur Musik der Dreigroschenoper," *Dreigroschenbuch,* pp. 184ff.
75   cf. Lotte Lenja's reminiscences in the booklet issued with the recording, p. 8

autonomous within it, there is no attempt to absorb them all into one experience. They are left rather to complete one another, and it is precisely in this "completeness" that Brecht sees the value of the procedure.

IV

Mahagonny falls naturally into three sections:

1. *Scenes 1–7,* which have the character of an exposition, an introduction of the characters and the motives which are to determine the "Spielraum" of what follows;
2. *Scenes 8–12,* which deal with Paul's revolt and the ensuing hurricane;
3. *Scenes 13–20,* which present an overall picture of Paul's anarchistic "paradise," as seen in its "four last things" — "Fressen, Liebe, Boxen, Saufen" — and of his downfall at the hands of his own system, as a result of his inability to pay. The "catastrophe" grows naturally out of the demonstration of "Boxen" and "Saufen"; Paul loses his money in a bet on Joe, but nevertheless feels obliged to stand drinks all round which he cannot pay for. The system then extracts the penalty from him, destroying itself in the process. It is, above all, this section of the play which encourages a comparison with the "Mysterienspiel" in its schematic demonstration of these "last things" and the dependence of everything on money.

The action of the opera really begins in Scene 8 with Paul's discovery that "etwas fehlt," that the "promised land" is not as it should be. Begbick's first "paradise," as we have seen, is based on a number of prohibitions which Paul reacts strongly against with the old cliché of "nothing ever happens" — the "Ruhe und Eintracht" of *Mahagonny,* the passive plainsong of the other three, is for him simply boredom. In his song he expresses the whole itchy restlessness of the twenties:

> Ihr habt gelernt das Cocktail-Abc
> Ihr habt den Mond die ganze Nacht gesehn
> Geschlossen ist die Bar von Mandelay
> Und es ist immer noch nichts geschehn.[76]

This urge to rebel, "seinen Hut aufzuessen," is held firmly in check by the "collective" of the other three (like the three of *Mann ist Mann,* or, later, the three agitators of *Die Maßnahme*) with a gently persuasive logic:

> Wir schlagen dich einfach nieder
> Ach, Paule, bis du wieder
> Ein Mensch bist!

76 GW 2, p. 519

Paul "will gar kein Mensch sein"; he is not prepared to accept this kind of existence. Any change is for him an improvement. He carries in him the seed of discontent with these eminently bourgeois pleasures; again the Alaska/Augsburg theme enters, the Odyssey of Paul/Brecht in search of gratification after the years of "Provinz" in Augsburg.

Scene 9 opens with a direct parody of this "Spießer"-like existence: the piano plays "Gebet einer Jungfrau," a cloud traverses back and forth, the "Hier-Darfst-Du-Schenke" is covered with prohibitions designed to preserve "Ruhe und Eintracht":

> Schonen Sie gefälligst meine Stühle
> Machen Sie keinen Krach
> Vermeiden Sie anstößige Gesänge[77]

To stress the "Kitschcharakter" of the scene we have in the first version Jakob's sigh of contentment and awe as the "Gebet einer Jungfrau" reaches a rather tinny climax: "Das ist die ewige Kunst." For Paul, the aggressive hero, the "Vatermörder," this is too much like home, the city of "Ruhe und Eintracht" has turned out to be a fair imitation of the middle-class pleasures of Augsburg.

In Scene 9 Paul's revolt is again opposed by a "collective," but for a wide variety of reasons. Jakob, Heinrich und Joe are genuinely concerned for his safety, but unable to understand the purpose of his revolt; Jenny and the six girls are merely carrying out their prescribed function (cf. Scene 10: "Jenny: Sei ruhig, Paule! Was redest du? / Geh hinaus mit mir und liebe mich.") Begbick, Fatty and Moses see a threat to the success of their "business" in Paul's rebellion; it is not their "Ruhe und Eintracht" that they are worried about, but their income. The men of Mahagonny join the opposition out of an incurable, "spießerisch" conservatism which characterises their utterances throughout the opera and gives the lie to Begbick's words: "Denn es ist die Wollust der Männer / Nicht zu leiden und alles zu dürfen." They have grown so passive that they cannot conceive of the existence of a freedom which they do not miss; they make no attempt to influence the course of events, but, as if following the advice of Jakob's song, "bleiben sitzen und warten auf das Ende." Paul, in a rather old-fashioned way, is determined to be the master of his own fate, he jumps onto the table and, with his rejection of "Ruhe und Eintracht," "invokes" the hurricane. He summons up an anarchy which is not merely "Grund der gegenwärtigen Ordnung" but "Grund jeglicher Ordnung": "die blinde Natur," or as Adorno also calls it, "das amorphe Sein," dominated by a "Selbstvernichtungstrieb" reminiscent of Freud. Paul sees the urge of self-gratification ("Spaß") as a "Naturgewalt" more powerful than the hurricane:

[77] GW 2, p. 520

Wozu braucht's da einen Hurrikan?
Was ist der Taifun an Schrecken
Gegen den Menschen, wenn er seinen Spaß will? [78]

Because the hurricane is only a "symbol," it disappears into thin air when its
function has been taken over by Paul's "Gesetze der menschlichen Glückseligkeit." The circle it makes round Mahagonny is of course a fiction; it is clear that
this hurricane was meant for Mahagonny and nowhere else and that it has merely
changed its form. It has been replaced as destructive principle by "der Mensch,
der seinen Spaß will." This conjunction of "Spaß" and "Zerstörung" is very
much more basic to Mahagonny than the criticism of an existing order. It is the
really radical "Aussage" of the opera which seems to disturb equally critics of
the bourgeois and Marxist persuasions. The "Gewalt" that Paul has discovered is
not merely a "Begleiterscheinung" of late capitalism, it is the basic anarchy of
human wishes which makes any form of society questionable, Marxist or
capitalist. The real difficulty for an orthodox Marxist critic in Mahagonny is not
that Paul, an "Arbeiter," should be the apostle of anarchy – he is in any case far
more an "adventurer" in the sense of the early poems than an "Arbeiter" – but
that the "anarchy" of Mahagonny is something more than an expression of
"bourgeois decadence." Brecht postulates here a universe which develops in a
diametrically opposed direction to Marxism, which turns the Hegelian dialectic
upside-down (or right-side up) far more radically than Marx. It is a kind of
dialectic with reversed sign, denying any possibility of "positive" progress, of a
"Weltgeist" which tends to the eventual good of humanity, whether ideal or
concealed as a "Naturgesetz." The progression is rather in the direction of the
antithesis; in this "negative" dialectic of Brecht's the basic anarchy of society
becomes increasingly conscious and gradually destroys the world about it. It is a
progression from an original lost unity, where the forces of decay and anarchy
are still unconscious and undeveloped, to a general "Weltungergang." Unlike
Hegel, Brecht sees the motive force of his "dialectic" in the gradual emergence
of this consciousness of decay and anarchy, which destroys the original
quasi-stasis and starts off the inevitable process of "Selbstvernichtung." This
process is mirrored in the structure of Mahagonny itself: in the first section of
the opera the false "Ruhe und Eintracht" is maintained because the destructive
powers lie dormant; Paul, however, discovers the "worm in the rose" and starts
the action spiralling towards its inevitable end. He discovers the essential
impossibility of any "Ruhe und Eintracht," that in the last analysis, "blinde
Natur herrscht." This, then, is a point of view above and beyond politics, a
position of philosophic pessimism which establishes a predetermined, fatalistic
"Weltuntergang," a perpetual worsening of the human condition which makes

---

[78] GW 2, p. 526

politics irrelevant and useless. There is no "proof" for the "optimistic" direction of Marx's and Hegel's systems (a study of history might seem, indeed, to support rather the opposite view); yet equally, it is hardly susceptible of disproof. In the same way, one can scarcely deny the tenability of a "dialectic" such as that of the early Brecht or of Beckett, however much one may be prepared to criticise its "barrenness." Beckett's plays, indeed, seem to have pushed this progression so far with their increasing self-restriction that the point of origin itself has become finally unimportant, so much are they directed at attaining the final, impossible stasis.

Mahagonny, then, has not been spared, but condemned, by Paul, "ein Wesen vielleicht, das überhaupt nicht ganz in soziale Relationen eingeht, aber allesamt erschüttert: mit seinem Tod muß Mahagonny sterben, und wenig Hoffnung bleibt übrig."[79] The "Naturgesetz" of Mahagonny is money, money as the representation of human greed, the need for gratification which is inhibited by society but constantly breaks through to the surface. These "wish-dreams" are expressed nowhere more clearly than in Paul's "commandments":

> Wenn es etwas gibt
> Was du haben kannst für Geld
> Dann nimm dir das Geld.
> Wenn einer vorübergeht und hat Geld
> Schlag ihn auf den Kopf und nimm dir das Geld:
> Du darfst es!
>
> Willst du wohnen in einem Haus
> Dann geh in ein Haus
> Und leg dich in ein Bett.
> Wenn die Frau hereinkommt, beherberge sie.
> Wenn das Dach aber durchbricht, geh weg!
> Du darfst es!
>
> Wenn es einen Gedanken gibt
> Den du nicht kennst
> Denke den Gedanken.
> Kostet er dich Geld, verlangt er dein Haus:
> Denke ihn! Denke ihn!
> Du darfst es!
>
> Im Interesse der Ordnung
> Zum Besten des Staates
> Für die Zukunft der Menschheit

---

[79] Adorno, op.cit., p. 135

Zu deinem eigenen Wohlbefinden
Darfst du![80]

The irony of the last "stanza" is obvious; the pleasure principle which Paul is advocating will scarcely serve to uphold order in the community or lead humanity to a bright future. The actual contradiction, as so often in Brecht, is made more striking by its apparent omission. The "temptation to think" of the third stanza is significant for the direction of the opera — thinking is seen here not as a positive element, as in the later works, but as a anarchist pleasure. In *Mahagonny* Brecht himself is "thinking a thought" very much in this way — to its final consequence. The "idealistic dialectic" which he saw later in *Im Dickicht der Städte*[81] is typical also of *Mahagonny*, which pursues such a dialectic to its conclusion. Paul, like Garga and Shlink, is intent on laying bare the basis of his own existence and thereby forcing his life towards the inevitable end of his argument, death.

The Mozart parody with which Weill surrounds the "trial of fire and water" of the hurricane has a related function; it insinuates the same kind of anarchy into the world of Sarastro. The two armed men are replaced by the men of Mahagonny with their meaningless exhortations, and there is no triumphal close in a world of justice and truth, but rather the opposite. The "apparent solution" of the crisis has a similar formal irony; like the window entry and exit in Hindemith's *Hin und Zurück*[82] the return of death to the waters from which it came has a strangely mechanical quality, as if the action had suddenly been wound backwards. Unlike Hindemith, Brecht and Weill have already motivated this "take-over" by the form; it is merely a quick and satisfying way of disposing of a "machine" which is no longer necessary.

* * * *

By Scene 13, the stage has been cleared for the systematic "Entlarvung" of the "four last things" of Mahagonny which forms the most unified and developed complex in the opera. The choice of these four "occupations" is not as arbitrary as it might at first seem. If we take "Boxen" out of the context of the 1920's and understand it rather as exemplary for the "joys of battle," the discharge of submerged aggression in its various forms into society, we have, in a schematic form, the four primary gratifications. Brecht's principle remains the same in all four of the demonstrations; he makes them "spin faster" until the

[80] GW 2, p. 528—9
[81] *Bei Durchsicht meiner ersten Stücke*, GW 17, p. 949
[82] cf. Friedrich Herzfeld, *Musica nova*, Berlin 1954, pp. 188ff.

absurdum is revealed, the impossibility of real gratification given the stranglehold of society over the individual.

"Fressen" is distorted into the "idyll" (in 1929, the prospect of three calves must have seemed paradisal enough to a large proportion of the audience); Jakob eats himself slowly to death to the accompaniment of a touching melody from the musicians. But the idyll is sarcastic; Jakob's hunger springs from his "Unersättlichkeit": "Ist es weg, dann hab' ich Ruh', / Weil ich es vergess . . . ," but even in death he is not brought to "Ruh": "Welch unersättlicher / Ausdruck auf seinem Gesicht ist." It is the impossible simplicity of Jakob's argument which is so "bestechend," but the death he seeks so singlemindedly fails to keep faith; like Paul, Jakob cannot become "satt."

"Der Liebesakt" (scene 14) is the most savage of Brecht's many satires of "modern love." In the first version the "title" appears in milder form, merely as "die Liebe," but one wonders if this too was not a result of the prudishness of Weill's publishers. In this brothel of "modern love," "Liebe, . . . ist doch an Zeit nicht gebunden" but the guests are requested to "move along, please": "Jungens, macht rasch, denn hier geht's um Sekunden." "Mandelay" is "vergänglich," the moon must be rationed so that the demand can be satisfied and the profit made. Begbick has modified her earlier statement, "Geld macht sinnlich," to "Geld allein macht nicht sinnlich," which conceals the real statement, "Ohne Geld keine Sinnlichkeit" under its brothel etiquette. Similarly, customers are asked to "Spucke den Kaugummi aus. / Wasche zuerst deine Hände. / Lasse ihr Zeit / Und sprich ein paar Worte mit ihr." This "etiquette," like the "Ruhe und Eintracht" of Scene 8, is designed to cover the sheer commercialism of the procedure with a coat of false romanticism. The opposition we saw in *Baal* between sensitivity and callousness is heightened here. Again, we can perhaps understand it best by a comparison with two roughly contemporary poems from the *Sonette*, "Entdeckung an einer jungen Frau" and "Kuh beim Fressen."[83] In fact, this cycle of sonnets contain Brecht's most personal utterances of any period; nowhere is it clearer that the radical disillusionment of *Mahagonny* springs from the intensity of his desire for a world without "Niedrigkeit und Bosheit," a desire for real "Größe" which cannot be satisfied in the alienated society in which he lives. The hardness, the scepticism and the provocation we meet throughout his early work are attempts to survive, to weather the constant battering to which his "subterranean sensitivity" is exposed.

"Entdeckung an einer jungen Frau" shows the origin of "Mandelay" in an attempt to challenge "time," a realisation of "Vergänglichkeit" and an attempt to oppose it by a feverish activity. Love, "die nicht an Zeit gebunden ist," is here confronted by time:

83 GW 8, pp. 160–1 and 162–3

Denn wir vergaßen ganz, daß du vergehst.

This realisation disturbs the tacit agreement of "hardness" between the two:

... eine Strähn in ihrem Haar war grau
Ich konnt mich nicht entschließen mehr zu gehen.

As in Mahagonny, time begins to "run out," and the consciousness of death expresses itself in a frantic effort to "die Gespräche rascher treiben." The desire which chokes the poet's voice is a protest against the imminent end of time, and at the same time a wish that it would come immediately and stop the process of decay. This desperation lies beneath the attack on the ideology of "Love" in the brothel scene; like Paul's attack on the "Ruhe und Eintracht" of Mahagonny, it springs from a total pessimism about the possibility of "Liebe" in a world dominated by the "negative dialectic." In the duet this despair is equally clear:

So mag der Wind sie in das Nichts entführen
Wenn sie nur nicht vergehen und sich bleiben
So lange kann sie beide nichts berühren[84]

It is this hopelessness which gives the "floating" diction of a poem such as "Erinnerung an die Marie A."[85] its curiously ambivalent and traumatic quality. The poet asks himself "Can this be so? ", and the answer is there, "Yes, it is so." It is a discovery which is made against his will, and yet he wills it. There is an astonishment at the extent to which the emotion has died, has worn itself out, a kind of strangely repressed "hurt." Of Marie A., only the cloud remains, she becomes the cloud; only the symbol of "die Vergänglichkeit der Liebe" has survived.

It may seem at first a little strange to refer to the sonnet "Kuh beim Fressen" in this context, but the "stummes Leiden" of the cow in this poem is almost exemplary for the sufferings of all Brecht's "heroines," the complete and hopeless passivity to which they are condemned, the great and necessary capitulation and the stoicism of a joyless survival. "Gewöhnt des Bösen," "sie duldet's stumm." "Sie will nicht wissen, was mit ihr geschieht." And so it is with Brecht's early heroines – from the start they have no chance, like Jenny, despite all the warnings of her "white mother." They simply wait, simply survive. Paul/Brecht has knowledge of this state; it drives him into the dualism of "Laßt uns die Gespräche rascher treiben," and "Wie langsam mir die kurze Zeit verrinnt." Unlike the women, he is not content to wait, he wants to make the world "spin faster," to remove the contradiction of "langsam" and "kurz." It is Brecht, not the cow, who "nützt die Abendstimmung aus"; his disillusioned

84   GW 2, p. 536
85   GW 8, p. 232

boredom gives way to an aggressive desire to make an end of it all, to hasten the process of "Beschmutzen" which he sees as the law of the world.

The two parts of Scene 14 are, then, despite all Brecht's strictures, less unrelated than they seem. In the brothel scene the desperation expresses itself more as aggression, as satire, in the duet it is more "private" in character, but it remains the same desperation and the same impatience. That this very beautiful poem should have been introduced into the opera at all, was perhaps a mistake, but it is indicative of the unifying power of the young Brecht's vision that it and the brothel scene do come together to form a curiously complete picture. Again, Weill's desperation matches Brecht's; the extraordinary bitonal writing for the violins in the last repetition of the Mandelay music has something of the quality of the wide spacing of Beethoven's late piano sonatas in the enormous gulf which opens in the music, as if it were being slowly driven apart by the "emptiness" in the middle. The more conventional pessimism of his world touches Brecht's in this lament for the "end of love." In Lenya's voice, in which "all his melodies came to him" and in which Lady Asquith heard "the voice of an innocent child singing outside a pub,"[86] there is the same "stummes Leiden," the same weary, tragic resignation of Brecht's heroines.

The brothel scene, like several of the *Sonette,* anticipates another major change in Brecht's attitudes: his rejection of the "sexualism" of his early work. Sexuality itself is seen as dominated and exploited by society, at best as a moment of forgetfulness as in "Die Liebenden," a forgetfulness which Brecht can no longer countenance in 1930. Even in 1927 we find him saying to Fritz Sternberg:

> Ich habe einmal ein Drama *Trommeln in der Nacht* geschrieben, und obwohl der Erste Weltkrieg [sic!] und die bayerische Revolution den Hintergrund bildeten, stand doch in diesem Drama die Beziehung eines Mannes zu einer bestimmten Frau im Mittelpunkt ... Seitdem ich dieses Drama geschrieben habe, ist es mir nicht mehr möglich, aus der Beziehung eines Mannes zu einer Frau eine Vision zu gewinnen, die stark genug wäre, ein ganzes Drama zu tragen.[87]

Brecht's later almost total rejection of the "pornographic" *Augsburger Sonette* is typical of this change, which was perhaps not uninfluenced by Helene Weigel, whom he married in 1928. A long period of silence on personal matters follows, and this particular sexual openness never returns; in the very charming and elegant sonnets of the early years in emigration it is replaced by an almost Augustan decorum. One poem survives, ensconced among examples of Brecht's

---

86 Quoted on the sleeve of the record "Lotte Lenya sings Berlin Theatre Songs"
87 Fritz Sternberg, *Der Dichter und die Ratio,* Göttingen 1963, p. 8

new "sociological" style, which seems to show this very process at work. It is the
last "confessional" poem of this kind he ever wrote:

>   Und er verglich nicht jene mit
>   Andern
>   Und auch nicht sich mit einem
>   Andern, sondern
>   Schickte sich an, bedroht, sich rasch zu
>   Verwandeln in
>   Unbedrohbaren Staub. Und
>   Alles
>   Was noch geschah, vollzog er wie
>   Ausgemachtes, als erfülle er
>   Einen Vertrag. Und ausgelöscht
>   Waren
>   Ihm im Innern die Wünsche.
>   Jegliche Bewegung
>   Untersagte er sich streng
>   Sein Inneres schrumpfte
>   Ein und verschwand, wie ein
>   Leeres Blatt entging er allem
>   Außer der Beschreibung.[88]

This poem is not only remarkable for its unusually lyric quality, but for its
analysis of a "Bedrohtsein" which is vital to an understanding of the works of
this period. Brecht is unable to attain a "Vision" from the "Beziehung eines
Mannes zu einer bestimmten Frau" sufficient to support a personality, let alone
a drama. He escapes from this "Bedrohung" of his personality into "Staub," by
turning himself into a "leeres Blatt" against which the "threat" is powerless.
Like the heroes of the later works, he survives in his "kleinste Größe," he
reduces himself to an unrecognisable anonymity, an existence as "No-one"
where he is no longer given away by his "self," and cannot be found to be
destroyed. In this poem, alone of all Brecht's descriptions of the search for "die
kleinste Größe," this search is presented explicitly as the result of a particular
relationship between man and woman. It is not our place to indulge in
biographical speculation, but it is clear that this poem, dating as it presumably
does from the late twenties, is very important indeed for an understanding of the

---

[88] Brecht, *Gedichte 2*, Frankfurt 1960, p. 171. I am at a loss to understand why this
poem has been omitted from the *Werkausgabe;* its unusually personal tone should scarcely
qualify it for the category of "zu wenig gesichert" (cf. GW 10, p. 30*), especially as the
motif of the "leeres Blatt" recurs in *Fatzer* (BBA 110/38) and is clearly related to the
"Niemand"-motif (see Chapter Two).

motives from which Brecht "changed his life" so radically at this time, and it is strange that it has been neglected by critics.

The *Sonette* and *Mahagonny* mark the end of Brecht's early preoccupation with sex. As Esslin notes,[89] when "love" reappears, it is in the guise of mother-love — even Grusche in *Der kaukasische Kreidekreis* is more characterised by her love for the royal child than for her lover Simon. The lovers of Brecht's early works are all "bedroht"; from "Die Liebenden" to "Entdeckung an einer jungen Frau," they have more than the "breath" of "Vergänglichkeit" on them, they can hope for no more than a moment's respite. The situation is from the first without hope:

> Wohin ihr? Nirgendhin. Von wem entfernt? Von allen.
> Ihr fragt, wie lange sind sie schon beisammen?
> Seit kurzem. Und wann werden sie sich trennen? Bald.
> So scheint die Liebe Liebenden ein Halt.[90]

In the later Brecht, the moment of "Vergessen" which is the unspoken ideal of the early poetry is consciously rejected as out of place in the outlook of a writer committed to the saving power of the human consciousness. Sexuality is treated simply as one of the "Genüsse" — in fact, Brecht is at great pains to assert the parity of others, such as eating, drinking, smoking and thinking. (Later it seems to disappear altogether in favour of "freundlich sein.") Mother-love becomes a symbol of "vernünftige Liebe," love which is based on foresight and considerateness, which is productive, in contrast to the "Liebe" of the early poems with its strong overtones of death-wish.

One cannot avoid the impression that the *Sonette* represent for Brecht a point beyond which it was impossible to go both in his work and in his life, and that the recognition of this on one level virtually implies the other. It is perhaps unfair to say that Brecht was no longer able to "live" what he could no longer write about, but we must see in this statement an interaction which remains true for him as a writer, and moved Peter Suhrkamp to claim even that "Brecht sei Kommunist geworden durch Kunst-Erfahrung."[91] The extraordinary tension of these sonnets is clear, not least between their chaotic content and the preciseness of the form into which it is conveyed. We should not underestimate the effect of this "sexual crisis" in the overall pattern of change in these years. The early work has a great unity of symbol and mood in this respect which we might almost call "pan-sexual"; with its rejection, Brecht destroys a whole world-picture. In rejecting Kragler, he rejects also Kragler's sexuality, which had managed to triumph over war and revolution, and that not only in *Trommeln in*

89 Esslin, op.cit., p. 346
90 GW 2, p. 536
91 Quoted by Max Frisch, *Theater heute,* November 1964, p. 1

der Nacht. In 1929 Brecht voluntarily castrates his art to avoid a recurrence of this betrayal. The sexuality of one man becomes unimportant in a world which is beginning to be dominated by Hitler. Paul, who combines the two sides of the Kragler-nature in a form almost as extreme as that of the *Sonette,* is clearly a transitional figure, so transitional indeed that he gains consciousness of his "mistake" between the two versions of the work. The farewell speech of the *Versuche* text is a farewell to Kragler, a farewell to the early Brecht, who dies with Mahagonny. Paul and Jenny are Kragler and Anna come to the end of the road:

> Paul: Nimm mir nichts übel.
> Jenny: Warum denn? [92]

In the process of learning "Einverständnis," of attaining the "kleinste Größe," the rejection of sexuality is one of the most important factors. It is significant that this rejection, this "purge," is carried out suddenly and without explanation; from this particular anonymity Brecht never again emerges. The very violence of the change lends ground to the theory that it has a central importance. There are few examples of such a complete volte-face — even poets like Dr. Donne who atoned for their wild youth in *Holy Sonnets* were generally able to transfer much of their technique and imagery to the Divine Bridegroom. Marxist-Leninism required a rather different approach.

* * * *

Scene 15 brings about Paul's downfall. At this point the demonstration of the last two "virtues" of Mahagonny becomes subservient to the demands of the plot. Joe finds his "fulfilment" as (un-) surely as Jakob, but his appeal to Paul's loyalty is the beginning of the end. Paul breaks his own "Gesetze": such a loyalty belongs not to the world after the hurricane, but to the world of Alaska/Augsburg, the vision of male camaraderie we discussed in relation to *Baal.* For Mahagonny it is an atavism, and is punished accordingly. The brutality of the fight anticipates the clown-scene of the *Badener Lehrstück vom Einverständnis.* Brecht's parody of the Alaska-motif seems here at its most bitter; "loyalty" becomes the assisting of one's friends in their projects of self-destruction. It is hard to avoid reading a sense of increasing isolation from his earlier friends into it, an isolation which springs from the realisation "Wie der Mensch dem Menschen hilft."[93]

92   GW 2, p. 557
93   cf. GW 2, pp. 592ff.

In Scene 16 the contradiction finally comes to the surface. Paul, in the process of demonstrating the fourth and last "thing" of Mahagonny, "Saufen laut Kontrakt," becomes "kontraktbrüchig" — he has no money. The fundament of paradise on earth is shattered:

Denn die Häute, die sind billig, und der Whisky, der ist teuer.[94]

"Völlig betrunken," Paul stages an imaginary escape from demands for payment, an escape which parodies all the "Utopias" from *Baal* on in a charade on a billiard table. The total bankruptcy of this Utopian illusion is expressed in a self-parody which reduces the world of the early adventurers to ships built of curtain rods and servant girls' songs. The "schwarze Wälder" of Alaska are an illusion, the storm is the reality. It is the "Gewalt," the anarchy on which Mahagonny is built, the hurricane which re-emerges to claim its victim. Paul's "Utopia," his desire to turn the clock back to a state before consciousness, is, as we have seen, itself at the root of his disaster. Nowhere is it clearer that the voyage to Utopia is really a voyage backward, that poor B. B. really wants to be carried back to the "schwarze Wälder" in his "Mutterleib" "wo man schlief und war da." But the reality is Mahagonny and the reckoning which no one will pay for him, not Jenny, not Heinrich. Jenny's song, in which she justifies her action, has a strange irony — she gets "getreten" as much as anyone else. The anarchist cannot, in the long run, avoid the consequences of his own anarchy reflected in others, nor is passivity a solution; the end overtakes it as surely as the other:

Wer in seinem Kober bleibt
Braucht nicht jeden Tag fünf Dollar
Und falls er nicht unbeweibt
Braucht er auch vielleicht nichts extra.
Aber heute sitzen alle
In des lieben Gottes billigem Salon.
Sie gewinnen in jedem Falle
Doch sie haben nichts davon.[95]

The "Genüsse" themselves have lost all content, "das Fleisch ist faul."

Scene 17 serves as a bridge to the trial scene. In it, the remains of the "culinary opera" are to be seen — it is clearly included merely to give Paul the opportunity for an aria.

Scene 18 begins the third act of the opera. In many ways, it anticipates the "Gerichtszene" of the later Brecht in the parallelism of the two completely dissimilar cases to be tried (as in *Der Kaukasische Kreidekreis*, years later), in its "Überschrift" ("Die Gerichte in Mahagonny waren nicht schlechter als andere

94 GW 2, p. 542
95 GW 2, p. 547

Gerichte") and in the conscious drawing of radically opposed conclusions from identical arguments, all procedures related very closely to later "Verfremdungs-effekte." The distortion of justice reveals its "Grund" — like "Liebe," like "Ruhe und Eintracht," it is only to be had for money.

The court's memory is long. Paul is charged with every one of his actions since his arrival in Mahagonny as a crime, despite the fact that the "Gerichtshof" itself was instrumental in most and has profited from all but his last, his failure to pay. Even the men of Mahagonny refuse to accept Moses' accusation of Paul:

> Aber in der gleichen Nacht
> Hat dieser Mensch sich aufgeführt
> Wie der Hurrikan selbst
> Und hat verführt die ganze Stadt
> Und vernichtet Ruhe und Eintracht![96]

"Es meldet sich kein Geschädigter." It is only when the evil trinity of Begbick, Fatty and Moses announce themselves as the plaintiffs whom Paul's action has "harmed" that he is lost. But in the process Moses has shown that all the values of Mahagonny are as split as "Ruhe und Eintracht," that the only unambiguous fact is money, which is at the basis of all, and that Paul's lack of it is a crime against the existing order. Without money he cannot buy his anarchy; without money he has no freedom to act.

In the "Benares Song," the Utopian theme is once more presented and rejected. We have seen how this scene "opens the perspective" of the opera before the final phase, Paul's execution and the end of Mahagonny, and discussed the differences of the two versions in these last scenes. Whether Paul goes to his death "unbelehrt" or not, this sequence of three scenes has an effect of cumulative pessimism which has scarcely been exceeded, even by Beckett and Arrabal. Mahagonny is hell and there is no heaven; Paul's "search" is an illusion. "Der wahrhaft Suchende wird enttäuscht." The opera attains the consciousness of "Der Nachgeborene": "Die Blinden reden von einem Ausweg. Ich / Sehe." A total reckoning is presented to the world of Mahagonny and its hero, the young Brecht, who dies here with Christ-parody in the midst of a sea of self-destroying confusions and contradictions. The violence of this burial is astonishing, its attempt to bring everything to an end without the slightest hope that something may arise from the ashes. *Mahagonny* buries a whole age and a whole age of Brecht. To have reached the point: "Können uns und euch und niemand helfen"[97] is to have demanded the destruction of a society and of a way of seeing it. Kragler wanted to destroy the theatre which was the world and escape into forgetfulness, but Paul has become judge and victim in one.

---

96 GW 2, p. 552
97 GW 2, p. 564

With Mahagonny and Paul, Brecht has destroyed the possibility of his early "vision," that of an individual able to carry a drama, able to attain the "Größe" he demands so constantly of literature and life. The easy relationship between writing and "Spaß" is over, the system no longer has the possibility of movement, and it is time to look for an Archimedean point. Brecht has reached that part of the spiral where movement is no longer significant, where the end is close and has been realised in almost full consequence, but the progression towards it becomes painfully slow, since little can be added to the end-consciousness already present. He has the choice whether, like Beckett, to concentrate ever more minutely on this brink of consciousness, to write end-game after end-game (and games they are, because the "rules," the conditions are so inflexible, like a patience which never works out), to analyse in each work a further narrowing development; or to "jump off," to try to deny the inevitability of the spiral, to reject the limitation it imposes, the single state of being, to destroy the individual Baal/Brecht who has become caught in this progression, bury him like Galy Gay and start again as "someone else." This "Ummontieren," pre-figured in *Mann ist Mann,* becomes for Brecht a necessity for survival, the retreat to the "kleinste Größe" which is an attempt to disappear into the "point of origin" and come out on the positive side of the axis (our spiral has become a helix). The perception of the absurdity and nothingness of the world leads to a new development which cannot reject the basic consciousness of this meaninglessness but attempts to confront it with a new, "thought" direction and to pull the world after it in this direction. Such a reversal demands the apparent rejection of an insight which has been gained and of the personality which gained it, a personality whose end is in self-destruction, and the substitution of their contraries by an act of hope.

But perhaps the problem of philosophical justification becomes secondary here to the problem of "fruitfulness," the problem of "going on." The author of the "Sonett über schlechtes Leben" cannot go on living *or* writing in this way; his impatience with the stasis to which he is reduced is the enemy of his own insight. The end will not come to him of itself, he must either remain becalmed in the stasis of this end-state, or desert a progression which can produce nothing more for him. At this stage, for Brecht, the demands of life and art seem to converge.

CHAPTER TWO

I

O ihr Knäblein, warum habt ihr mich statt Galy
Gay damals nicht gleich noch Garniemand ge-
nannt?

Mann ist Mann, Scene 11.[1]

Mann ist Mann is the most problematic of all Brecht's early plays; the mass of
material in the Brecht-Archiv, into which Marianne Kesting, in a recent article,[2]
has bravely tried to introduce a semblance of order, is sufficient evidence that
Brecht himself was well aware of these problems. The attempted "Zurücknahme" which we have discussed in relation to *Mahagonny* is even more obvious
here; there is no doubt that in the earlier versions, Brecht intended Galy Gay's
"Ummontierung" to be seen in a positive light, and that it was only later that he
became aware of the need to alienate the audience's sympathy from this
"Wachstum ins Verbrecherische." A typed addition to the "Propyläen" version
of 1926 in the Brecht-Archiv lets the play end on the following unambiguous
note:

Da marschieren sie hin
der neue Mann immer voran
einmal war er Galy Gay der Packer
aber dann wurde er verwandelt
er wurde dadurch stärker
Jetzt hat er schon eine Bergfestung
erobert und niemand weiss, was
morgen sein wird.
Mann ist Mann
Aber der "Neue" Mann
ist der bessere Mann[3]

The concept of "der neue Mann [Mensch]" is of central importance in Brecht's
work in these years; in her "Notizen über Brechts Arbeit 1926" Elisabeth
Hauptmann tells of his plan to follow the *Hauspostille* with "eine andere
Sammlung, die sich mit dem neuen Menschen befaßt."[4] The poetry of the

---

[1] GW 1, p. 374
[2] "Die Groteske vom Verlust der Identität: Bertolt Brechts 'Mann ist Mann'," *Das deutsche Lustspiel,* II. Teil, ed. H. Steffen, Göttingen 1970, pp. 180ff.
[3] BBA 313/125
[4] loc.cit.

period is full of the consciousness of a revolutionary change in literature and humanity, of the emergence of a "new man" and a new literature which will render the old forms as obsolete as the motor car the horse. The poem "Alles Neue ist besser als alles Alte"[5] expresses this conviction in a particularly brash way. The term "der neue Mann" has, of course, strong Expressionistic overtones, but Brecht uses it in a sense which corresponds rather to the mood of "die neue Sachlichkeit"; it belongs, in his work, to a phase of "technologism" (often connected with things American) which has left many traces, especially, as we shall see, in *Der Flug der Lindberghs*. A text from the late twenties describes this new consciousness with considerable objectivity:

> Kurz nach dem grossen krieg schien uns jungen leuten eine neue zeit angebrochen — anhörend die neue amerikanische musik betrachtend die fotografien der grossen städte konnten wir nicht mehr zweifeln: die neue zeit war gekommen, grösser als jede vorhergehende, und wir waren bestimmt unser einmaliges leben in ihr zu verbringen. diese zeit schien uns nicht in sonne getaucht dieses leben schien uns kaum leicht im gegenteil: von grosser härte und ausserordentlicher kühnheit. im bilde dieses geschöpfes unserer einbildungskraft störte uns nicht ungerechtigkeit noch grausamkeit.[6]

Brecht's attitude to the "neue zeit" seems at first curiously ambivalent: it leads him, on the one hand, to rather futuristic eulogies of progress, on the other, to apocalyptic visions of the type we have discussed in Chapter One. The two aspects are combined in a fragment from *Die Sintflut:*

> in den jahren der flut verändern sich die menschentypen das ist die grösste zeit die die Menschheit erlebt hat (die typen werden stärker grösser finsterer sie lachen ... in den letzten jahren verbreiten sich seuchen von ungeheuren erfindungen flugmenschen treten auf sie gelangen zu grösserem ruhm als je zuvor menschen
>
> sie fallen ins wasser gelächter[7]

The ambivalence of technologism and apocalypse is more apparent than real. This "Fieber des Städtebaus und des Öls"[8] in which humanity is to attain its apogee is only the last "fling" before the "Sintflut"; "der neue Mensch" is also "der letzte Mensch."

Brecht's protagonists in the mid-twenties fit clearly into this development; they reject the old forms of behaviour as no longer fitting to "die neue zeit" and seek to acquire the "grosse härte" and "ausserordentliche kühnheit" it demands

---

5 GW 8, p. 314
6 BBA 460/63
7 BBA 214/17
8 cf. GW 2, p. 591

of them. Curiously enough, however, it is only Galy Gay who fully succeeds in making this adjustment; the others are destroyed, at the last moment, by an atavistic element in their characters which exposes them to their fate. Galy alone is able to become totally "der neue Mensch," and this despite his apparent weakness, his "weiches Gemüt" and his inability to say no. He is systematically stripped of his old personality until he is not only the equal, but the master of his environment.

Yet Galy's transformation is in no sense the prelude to a new social order, Communistic or otherwise; it is simply a radical realisation of Baal's strategy, the art of being "asozial in einer asozialen Gesellschaft." The "Ungerechtigkeit" and "Grausamkeit" of society must be met on their own terms, and Galy is merely more successful than Brecht's other early heroes in ridding himself of surfaces for attack. His passage through the "Nullpunkt" of "Niemandsein" thus differs radically from the superficially similar process we shall be analysing in the Badener Lehrstück, though, as we shall see, it can tell us a great deal about the motivation of this later "Auslöschung der Persönlichkeit." Unlike the three "Monteure" of the Lehrstück, he does not surrender his personality in order to submit himself to the will of a benevolent historical process, he merely replaces it by another, which is more suited to his environment. The environment, however, remains that of Mahagonny and Die Sintflut; its "newness," its modernity, is not a beginning, but an end. Galy's "fame" will, we feel, like that of the "Flugmenschen" of Die Sintflut, be followed by a "Fall ins Wasser" and the sardonic laughter of the prophet of the end of time.

Nevertheless, this "change of personality" is of enormous importance for an understanding of Brecht's personal development in these years. We have seen that, in the early plays and poems, the motif of "loss of consciousness" recurs constantly, as a desired retreat into a state of pre-conscious unity, and have interpreted this as an attempt on Brecht's part to escape from an environment which threatens his "subterranean" sensitivity, the "weiches Gemüt" beneath the elephant hide he has been forced to adopt. In Mann ist Mann this "inner personality" is systematically eliminated, so that Galy may become all impregnable elephant. His integration into the group is understood by Brecht at first in an entirely positive sense; the essential ambivalence of his earlier heroes, their combination of "Weiche" und "Härte," is here polarised in the contrast of Galy's old and new personalities, and the old is summarily liquidated. Oddly enough, his passing of this test renders him stronger than the others; his new "Härte" is more radical and more secure than theirs since it is based on an existential insight into the irrelevance of "self" and the conscious adoption of a new "face" which corresponds to the demands the environment makes on him.

In Mann ist Mann the concept of "Niemandsein" and of the symbolic death which are to dominate Brecht's work during the crisis of the late twenties appear for the first time. Galy Gay's consciousness that he may as well have been called

"Garniemand" from the beginning is the pivot of the whole process and the secret of his ability to pass through it successfully. By reducing himself to his "kleinste Größe," the simplest level of humanity (cf. Begbick: "So einer ißt auch noch als Garniemand"[9]) he is able to survive the ritual destruction of his old self and emerge triumphantly as "die menschliche Kampfmaschine." Galy's transformation is contrasted further with Bloody Five's self-destructive clinging to the name and reputation which seem his only defence against the flood of sexuality which threatens to engulf him and rob him of his self (as we have seen, a motif of some autobiographical significance!). But it is useless to resist these depersonalising forces; Galy is the first of Brecht's heroes to realise that the answer lies in a kind of "Flucht nach vorn," a total surrender of the threatened personality which permits survival and clears the way for the "new man."

The relationship of this solution to the problems discussed in the last chapter is as obvious as it is, at least superficially, unsatisfactory. The unattainable end of the "Selbstvernichtungsprozeß" has been turned into a kind of "Jungbrunnen"; "das ertrunkene Mädchen" reemerges as an Amazon! The point on which the gyres of the helix have been converging is shown not as an end, but as a transition; the helix emerges on the "other side" as a new "reborn" self which has apparently freed itself from the old compulsion. This "Nullpunkt," which we may perhaps be forgiven for calling the "point of origin," in view of its regressive connotations in the early work, proves to be only a metaphorical death, not an actual one; it corresponds, in the play, to the faint into which Galy falls whilst he is being "shot." The problem of preserving one's identity in the face of a hostile environment is solved, sophistically enough, by surrendering it; a new "self" appears which is suddenly able to master the world about it.

Much as this whole process may at first seem a kind of philosophical sleight of hand, the radical volte-face which Galy represents in Brecht's work is of vital significance. His "weiches Gemüt," as we have seen, is subliminally present in most of Brecht's early heroes, but it is generally rejected in favour of an egocentric asociality which tries to beat society at its own game. The real advance in *Mann ist Mann* is the realisation that this strategy was "upside-down," that it is precisely "das Weiche" which in the long run survives and conquers (a theme Brecht was later to develop memorably in his poem on Laotse). The polarity Galy — Fairchild shows quite clearly the superiority of Galy's tactics, and it is a lesson which the author can scarcely have forgotten.

The works I shall be discussing in this chapter are all centrally concerned with the elimination of an "old," inadequate personality and its replacement by a new, Marxist-influenced consciousness of the relationship between individual and collective, which subjects the traditional concept of "personality" to a rather drastic critique. The "old" personality is represented by a series of related

9   GW 1, p. 357

characters (Baal, Nungesser, Fatzer) who are all "alter egos" of the young Brecht, much as Paul Ackermann had been; the new consciousness is expressed most clearly in the figure of Herr Keuner, "der Denkende," of whom more anon. It seems clear that Brecht's main purpose in these plays is fundamentally self-educative, to eliminate systematically the Baal-Fatzer personality he had been cultivating for years and replace it with a new Keunerian consciousness. In the course of our discussion of *Fatzer, Das Badener Lehrstück* and *Der böse Baal der asoziale* I shall support this identification more fully, but it is important to realise at this point that *Mann ist Mann* shows the necessity (and practicability?) of such a transformation *before its political aim has even been formulated;* Galy Gay changes, not because the revolution demands it, but because he must change to survive. In Chapter One we saw that this problem had reached a stage of considerable acuteness for Brecht in 1925; *Mann ist Mann* proves conclusively that it is not fundamentally a political problem, but a psychological one, and that his "conversion" to Marxism in the late twenties had already been pre-figured, in an embarrassingly neutral fashion, in Galy Gay's absorption into the "negative" collective of an imperialist army — Brecht's alterations to the play for the 1931 production, which attempt to show this process, or rather its result, in a negative light, serve only to confuse the issue; Galy's "changeability" remains an exemplary strategy of survival, whether he is turned into a "Schlächter" or not, and a critique of the play from a Marxist point of view must surely reject not only the "wrong collective," but Galy's "Einverständnis," which allows him to be absorbed into it so easily. Clearly Brecht intended to give the play an anti-Fascist direction in 1931, but (as so often) his revisions seem incompatible with the basic tendency of the work which survives despite them. Galy's adaptability cannot have its sign changed quite so simply, and indeed, it remains characteristic of all Brecht's later "heroes." The ambivalence of his "strategy of survival," which springs, at this stage, more from a private, psychological necessity than from a recognition of the historical role of the collective, becomes a central problem in the later work.

In *Mann ist Mann* we meet for the first time a particular formal device which recurs constantly in the following plays; the schematic representation of the relationship between individual and society in terms of the "group of four." This motif is repeated, as we have seen, in *Mahagonny,* in Paul's relationship to the other three "Holzfäller"; it is employed again in *Fatzer,* in the *Badener Lehrstück,* and finally in *Die Maßnahme.* It is as if Brecht were attempting in these plays to analyse all possible inter-relationships on the basis of an almost mathematical "Modell"; in the course of the argument, the wheel turns full circle, from Galy's absorption into a "wrong" collective to the rejection of "der junge Genosse" by the "right" collective. In *Mahagonny,* the collective of *Mann ist Mann* is broken up again by Paul's relapse into "individualism" and his recognition of the false basis of such a collective, whose "order" is only a mask designed to cover the naked force on which it is based; the essential contradiction of *Mann ist Mann*, which creates a "new man" but fails to integrate him into a new society, is exposed, and consequently Brecht reverts, in *Mahagonny*, to an even more extremely nihilistic view of the world. The emergence of a new breed of "hero" ("stärker, größer, finsterer"), does nothing to halt the "Weltuntergang," in fact, it gives it new momentum, since the logical goal of this new heroism is to hasten the apocalypse and endure it stoically, like the prophet Nahaia in *Die Sintflut*. In *Fatzer*, the emphasis has shifted once more to the power of the collective and the use it is to make of the individual Fatzer; in the course of a number of versions, Brecht finally arrives at the conclusion that Fatzer's egoism is socially worthless and liquidates him in favour of Keuner, who is introduced as a "Gegenspieler" only in the last stages of composition. In *Das Badener Lehrstück*, this process is continued; the egoistical Nungesser is "driven out," while the three "Monteure" are able to survive the passage through their "kleinste Größe," to become "no-ones," and then re-emerge as members of the "good" collective. In *Die Maßnahme*, this collective exists from the start and rejects one of its members who relapses into "individualism." In the course of these plays, then, not only has the character of the collective been completely reversed from a "Maschinengewehrabteilung" of the British army to a group of Communist agitators helping to bring the revolution to China, but the relationship of the individual to it has undergone an extraordinary change; from Galy Gay's neutral "Einverständnis" through Paul's and Fatzer's anarchistic rebellion to the positive "Einverständnis" of the "Monteure" and the "wrong" rebellion of Nungesser and the "junger Genosse." However problematical Brecht's first exposition of the theorem may be in *Mann ist Mann*, it is clear that it came to dominate his thoughts during the period and to provide the framework within which the argument which he was conducting with himself in these years could be worked out. His statement on *Fatzer*, "so ist das fatzerdokument zunächst hauptsächlich zum lernen des schreibenden gemacht,"[10] could be extended to cover this whole phase of his work.

10 BBA 109/14

II

Schwach sein ist menschlich und drum muß es
aufhören
Fatzer[11]

Of all Brecht's unpublished fragments, *Fatzer*, or to give it its full title,
Untergang des Egoisten Johann Fatzer, is the most nearly complete, the most
significant and the most important for an understanding of his development, and
it is a tragedy that it remains almost entirely unpublished. Elisabeth Hauptmann
and Emil Burri had planned an edition some years ago, but with Burri's death
the project was set aside, until Reiner Steinweg, in a doctoral disseration on
Brecht's "Lehrstücke"[12] which, with Dieter Schmidt's *Baal* edition,[13] represents
perhaps the single most important contribution to Brecht studies over the last
ten years, set himself the task of ordering the material and establishing the
sequence of the many versions. One can only hope that Steinweg will soon be
entrusted with a full edition of the *Fatzer* material, which must necessarily bring
about an almost total revision of our picture of Brecht's development in these
years. My discussion of *Fatzer* in this chapter is based on my own reading in the
Archiv and on Steinweg's dissertation; although it is obviously somewhat
unsatisfactory to base a section of this analysis of Brecht's work in the late
twenties and early thirties on material which is not generally accessible, there
seems, at present, little alternative.

It is difficult to summarise the "plot" of *Fatzer* in view of the many, often
conflicting versions; the argument of the play was so vital to Brecht that he
returned to it again and again, and there is evidence that he never gave up the
idea of "completing" it. However, a "skeleton" common to all versions might .
read as follows:[14]

A group of four soldiers desert their tank during the first World War and
make for Mühlheim, where they find a hiding-place with the wife of one of their
number. Fatzer, who was the prime mover in their desertion, is their "leader"
figure; but he proves unworthy of their trust. Instead of finding food for them,
he becomes involved in a personal feud with the butchers; he seduces his friend's
wife while the others are absent, and finally betrays them to the authorities.
They, however, condemn Fatzer to death for his anti-collective behaviour, and

[11] BBA 109/80
[12] Reiner Steinweg, *Brechts Lehrstück. Untersuchung eines Theorie-Praxis Modells*,
Diss. Kiel 1969. (See also Introduction, Note 1)
[13] *Baal. Drei Fassungen*, Frankfurt 1966; *Baal, Der böse Baal der asoziale. Texte,
Varianten, Materialien*, Frankfurt 1968. See also Dieter Schmidt, *"Baal" und der junge
Brecht*, Stuttgart 1966.
[14] cf. Steinweg (diss.), pp. 136ff.

carry the sentence out before they themselves are overtaken by their inevitable fate.

The names of the characters change considerably from version to version, but two remain fairly stable; Fatzer, the "egoist" who is incapable of adjusting himself to the demands of a collective, and Koch/Keuner, who progresses in the course of the play's composition from a kind of apostle of natural justice, who wishes for once to rebel against the proverb "es wird nicht so heiß gegessen, wie gekocht wird"[15] to an incarnation of the new Marxist ethic of the collective. The real conflict takes place between these two adversaries, and in the "Keuner" version Brecht finally achieves the confrontation of "old" and "new" selves in a form which makes its relevance to the central problems of this stage of his development abundantly clear.

Brecht's identification of Fatzer with his old self, Baal-Brecht, is unusually explicit. Not only does Fatzer's characterisation echo Baal's in almost every detail, but Brecht even presents him with lines from the "Sonnet über schlechtes Leben,"[16] and, as if this were not clear enough, attaches a photo of himself, taken in Augsburg in 1927, to a page of the text in which Koch demands Fatzer's "Ausmerzung" under the charming motto: "schwach sein ist menschlich und drum muß es aufhören."[17] Fatzer's "weakness" must be stopped, because it can be put to no use by the new collective:

> und wo ein fluß war der sehr stark stank und wo
> leute standen und sagten: heute
> ist er wieder voll von stinkendem Öl oder heute
> ist er giftgrün oder jetzt wieder klarer
> da soll kein besserer fluß mehr fließen sondern
> kein fluß mehr. so
> soll dieser fatzer auch kein besserer oder schlechterer fatzer
> sein sondern soll
> kein fatzer mehr sein[18]

From the point of view of Koch/Keuner's new "collective ethics," Fatzer is "völlig schlecht" and must be liquidated, even in the apparently hopeless situation of the play, in order that, at least for once, an "order" may be established which holds hope for the future.

Unlike Nungesser in the *Badener Lehrstück,* however, Fatzer is given ample opportunity to defend himself, and indeed, in his "Rede gegen den Sozialismus" we may well see the objections which Brecht himself had to overcome before turning to Marxism:

15   BBA 109/84
16   BBA 110/13
17   BBA 109/80
18   loc.cit.

was ihr nicht begreift ist die mechanik
eure ungesunde lust
wie räder zu sein
ich aber wills nicht
ich will aufpassen was sie machen
denn
es ist methode drin die sie nicht kennen
ich aber kenn sie
      / als sie sich säubern wollen für ihren Klassenkampf /
trät man ihnen mit einem stiefel
in die visagen sie merktens nicht
die haben visagen wie hornige hufe
sie werden nicht
viel anders sie sind
nichts als unzerstörbar ich aber
will nicht so sein[18a]

Fatzer, "der ichsüchtige,"[19] "das schöne Tier,"[20] "ist kein rad"; indeed, as Brecht writes elsewhere, he "holds up" the wheel of history,[21] he is an atavism which stands in the way of progress. His egoism rebels against the "mechanik" of the new ethics. The conflict between Fatzer and Keuner is perhaps illustrated most clearly in the scene "Fatzers zweite Abweichung" published by Brecht himself,[22] and a speech of Fatzer's in which he protests against the failure of the three to come to his aid. He has allowed himself to become involved in a brawl with the butchers who alone can provide the four with the meat they need to survive, and appeals to the others to help him. Keuner, however, holds them back, and disclaims any knowledge of Fatzer; he realises the danger of exposing all four of them to the police by this action. Fatzer reacts bitterly to this "disloyalty":

ihr wart recht klug
aber vielleicht zu klug?
standet ihr da und hattet eure muskeln in der hand?
solchen kann es nicht übel gehen.
so kluge leute brauchen niemand zum beistand.
höchstens könnte man sagen euch fehlt es
(nur um ein geringes)
an impulsiver zuneigung

18a BBA 111/02
19 BBA 109/18
20 BBA 110/28
21 BBA 109/63
22 GW 7, pp. 2901ff.

törichtem aufbrausen
vielleicht hättet ihr euch durch solche
unbeherrschtheit hineingeritten und
vielleicht wärt ihr auch wieder herausgekommen
vielleicht durch euren
von so viel zuneigung gerührten fatzer
aber das könnt ihr vielleicht auch nachholen
wenn auch ein kleiner schatten
bleibt, da man euch auf das,
was nur natürlich ist, die
nase stoßen muß.
kurz und gut: ich lad euch ein
teilzunehmen an meinem streit
        etwas unvernunft bitte![23]

    Yet it is his "disloyalty" which has brought about the situation, his failure to place the interests of the group above his private bellicosity. Fatzer is "der führer, welcher erpreßt / er geht zum feind über und muss erschlagen werden";[24] although he possesses unusual abilities, he is unwilling to put them in the service of others, but, like Jim/Paul in *Mahagonny,* follows his own anarchistic "laws of human happiness." As Brecht writes of him: "er kann etwas tun — dann muß er es tun — aber er kann es nicht tun müssen."[25] He is possessed by the fear of becoming merely a cog in the machine; in a vision of "der massenmensch" he returns to this "mechanical," depersonalised quality of the "new man:"

seine art ist mechanisch
    einzig durch bewegung zeigt er sich
jedes glied auswechselbar selbst die person
mittelpunktlos[26]

Fatzer is determined to resist the fate of Galy Gay, who is "wie ein Auto ummontiert," although he recognises clearly enough, like Jimmy Mahony, the hopelessness of his own existence, his "Vorläufigkeit." He is unable to surrender his "personality"; his egoism is his sole *raison d'être.* Confronted with the new ethics of Koch/Keuner, he laments his "Ausgestoßenheit" (cf. "die Austreibung" in the *Badener Lehrstück*):

ich bin ihnen wie ein fuss
der abgestorben am lahmen flechsen hängt

23 BBA 110/55
24 BBA 814/02
25 BBA 111/02
26 BBA 111/19

und den sie hinter sich herziehen ohne lust
ihn nur nicht abschneidend
weil sonst ihr blut rausläuft
aber
der teil von ihnen ist fühllos
darauf kann man treten ohne dass sie
au sagen und wiewohl sie mich brauchen
gibt mir keiner die hand sie schauen mich an
wie einen kranken.[27]

Yet, like Nungesser in the *Badener Lehrstück*, he is unable to learn his lesson and become a "no-one." Characteristically enough, he finishes by betraying the others, but accepts their challenge to submit himself to their judgment out of a sense of bravado.

The sexuality which Baal, in common with all Brecht's early heroes, had recognised as his great weakness, is also Fatzer's scourge. His first "Abweichung," the "seduction" of Therese Kaumann, is a clearly anti-social act, as the four depend on her for their safety, and it is their presence which has prevented her from relieving her frustrations with her husband. Fatzer, of course, "hat die frau über ehe er sie noch richtig hat."[28] In one version, he finds lodging with a prostitute after the others have thrown him out and, in a most Macheathian way, brings her with him to his "Urteil" (there is even provision for an "Eifersuchtsduett," "komm heraus, du schönheit von mühlheim"[29]). In the "Kommentar" which Brecht planned to attach to *Fatzer*, the "Geschlechtskapitel" has a prominent place; "das geschlechtliche," he writes, should be shown as "unnatürlich ... schmutzig, gefährlich und unverständlich,"[30] so that a proper respect for its dangers may be inspired in the young. Fatzer's sexuality is one of those human weaknesses which must "stop," if the new society is to emerge, and which correspond closely to the "four last things" of *Mahagonny;* "Fressen," "Saufen," "Boxen" and "Liebe."

The increasingly radical rejection of Fatzer's egoism which characterises the different versions of the text is counterbalanced by a corresponding "Aufwertung" of his opposite, Koch. At first, Koch's determination to create "order," even at the cost of life, seems more a variant of Brecht's early nihilism than a hope for the future, but in the later versions he comes more and more to stand for a new type of consciousness which, even if it is itself unable to bring about the desired change in society, foreshadows it. Significantly, in the "final" version, his name, which along with Fatzer's had been one of the few stable

27 loc.cit.
28 BBA 112/03
29 BBA 109/79
30 BBA 112/64

elements in the play, is changed to Keuner, and he is for the first time presented as a Marxist struggling to make the best of an impossible situation.[31] To understand the full significance of this change we must first examine the works in which the figure of Herr Keuner has its genesis, the *Geschichten vom Herrn Keuner* and the *Badener Lehrstück vom Einverständnis*.

III

Jetzt wißt ihr:
Niemand
Stirbt, wenn ihr sterbt.
Das Badener Lehrstück vom Einverständnis[32]

Herr Keuner's "alias" was first deciphered by Walter Benjamin in a study entitled *Was ist das epische Theater?* which remained unpublished until 1966. He terms Keuner "einen schwäbischen 'Utis,' ein Gegenstück zu dem griechischen 'Niemand' Odysseus, der den einäugigen Polyphem in der Höhle aufsucht."[33] This allusion was expanded brilliantly by Klaus Heinrich in an "Exkurs über Odysseus und Herrn K." in his *Versuch über die Schwierigkeit nein zu sagen*[34] (a very Brechtian title), to which I shall have cause to refer frequently in the next pages. Yet few critics seem to have realised how closely related this emergence of a "Mr. Nobody" in Brecht's work is to the central theme of the contemporary *Badener Lehrstück*, in which Herr Keuner in fact appears under another of his more frequent aliases, "der Denkende." I propose at this point to attempt a detailed interpretation of the *Lehrstück*, both for its importance to the central argument of this chapter and from a conviction that this difficult and obscure work has received far too little attention from critics, despite its obviously significant position in Brecht's development.

Like so many of Brecht's plays, *Das Badener Lehrstück vom Einverständnis* is itself a "correction" of an earlier play, the first of all Brecht's "Lehrstücke," *Der Flug der Lindberghs*, which he later saw fit to omit from the *Stücke* edition and, when approached in 1949 by the South German Radio for permission to perform the work as a radio play, retitled *Der Ozeanflug*, removing all reference to Lindbergh, an alteration which has been followed and "typographisch deutlich gemacht" in somewhat pedantic fashion in the reprint of *Versuche* Heft 1–4.[35] The reasons for Brecht's embarrassment are not hard to see; *Der*

31   cf. BBA 433/40
32   GW 2, p. 606
33   Benjamin, op.cit., p. 11
34   Frankfurt 1964
35   cf. *Versuche 1–4*, Frankfurt 1959, p. 355

Flug der Lindberghs, which we must assume to have been written soon after Lindbergh's crossing of the Atlantic and under the immediate impression of this achievement, expresses so naive a belief in "progress" that even the notes of the *Versuche* edition, dating presumably from 1929–1930, reveal a certain "distance" from the work.

This brief phase of what we might call "technological optimism" is one of the stranger aspects of Brecht's search for the "new man" (for which we have seen evidence from as early as 1926) and has left its mark on his work (the most obvious examples are the extraordinarily flat "machine poems," "Sang der Maschinen" and the three "Kranlieder"[36]). It seems to represent a kind of extreme point in his search for an "external" direction, a point at which he came close to "die neue Sachlichkeit" and to the belief in technological progress as a value in itself which had already formed an essential feature of Marinetti's Futurist Manifesto. It seems at first strange that a writer so dominated by the "end-consciousness" of *Mahagonny* should be capable of the banality of a title like "Alles Neue ist besser als alles Alte," yet surely this is in fact only an indication of the urgency of the need to "escape" – for Brecht, the new *is* better than the old because it may provide at least a temporary diversion from the stasis of *Mahagonny,* an illusion of movement. The Brecht who satirises the excesses of "die neue Sachlichkeit" in the poem "700 Intellektuelle beten einen Öltank an"[37] is himself by no means immune to excesses of this sort, nor is he as guiltless of the charge of creating "Leere mit Tempo" as his poem "Kleine Epistel, einige Unstimmigkeiten entfernt berührend"[38] attempts to make out. We have seen that the desire to make the world "spin faster" is a logical outcome of the "end-game," but here it is transferred bodily into a new world where its role seems, to say the least, doubtful – as a "mechanistic optimism" which seems over-simple and even slightly ridiculous. The unconcealed threat in the last line of this poem shows clearly how an attack on this weakest point in Brecht's armour could provoke him into an unfortunate exhibition of blustering. There is, after all, a certain doubt as to whether the work that Brecht was producing at this particular time is "history" in quite the same way as the building of the Suez Canal or of the Great Wall of China, but it is precisely this consciousness of being the "modern," the "dernier cri," which Brecht seems to need at this stage; after all, his nihilism becomes somewhat meaningless if he cannot pretend to have attempted all solutions and found them wanting. The arrogance which becomes the nihilist, who sees what others fail to see, that all their actions are useless, and is thus free from the necessity of suggesting other actions, sits less easily on the "optimist," who must justify his new plan for the world.

---

36 GW 8, pp. 297ff.
37 GW 8, p. 316
38 GW 8, p. 126

Despite occasional "socialist" overtones (the plural of the title, the emphasis on the role of those who had built Lindbergh's plane in his eventual success[39]), *Der Flug der Lindberghs* in its "Schlacht gegen das Primitive" tends strongly towards a simple glorification of Lindbergh as the "new man" and to a simplification of the historical role of science in "changing the world" which the author of *Leben des Galilei* would hardly have endorsed:

> So auch herrscht immer noch
> In den verbesserten Städten die Unordnung
> Welche kommt von der Unwissenheit und Gott gleicht.
> Aber die Maschinen und die Arbeiter
> Werden sie bekämpfen, und auch ihr
> Beteiligt euch an
> Der Bekämpfung des Primitiven![40]

Nevertheless, a number of its features survive in the later work. It is no coincidence that the *Badener Lehrstück* begins with the final speech of the earlier play, altered only slightly (if significantly); it could be said to "take over" where the other leaves off, to deal with the serious problems which had been avoided or ignored in the earlier work. After all, *Der Flug der Lindberghs* had been primarily intended for an audience of children. Both plays deal with airmen: the first has as its relatively unambiguous hero Charles Lindbergh himself, the second takes the failure of the French aviator, Charles Nungesser, whose name already appears in a "Szenenüberschrift" in the earlier play as a kind of "negative" for Lindbergh's triumph ("Unter sich den Schatten Nungessers"[41]), as its starting-point, but quickly distances itself from the historical source.

In many ways the *Badener Lehrstück* conforms to Brecht's practice in "completing and correcting" earlier works. In a truly dialectic spirit, he treats in Charles Nungesser the "negative" side of Lindbergh, the "technological hero" (Lindbergh himself was to become "negative" enough as far as Brecht was concerned through his "enge Beziehungen zu den Nazis"[42]), and by this "completion" corrects the over-simplifications of the earlier play and makes them appear in their true relativity. Typical is the substitution, on the one hand, of "das / Noch nicht Erreichte" for the earlier "das / Unerreichbare"[43] in the prologue, on the other hand, the working-out of the full questionability of the values of the "Lindberghs" in the figure of Nungesser. The *Badener Lehrstück* is at the same time more "accurate" in its optimism and in its realisation of the

39   cf. GW 2, p. 571
40   GW 2, p. 577
41   GW 2, p. 580
42   *Versuche 1—4*, loc.cit.
43   GW 2, p. 590

dangers of a "progress" which is not progress for mankind as a whole. Nungesser is a "Zurücknahme" of Lindbergh; his "flying" is seen as not good in itself, but only good if directed to the good of all, and, as it becomes increasingly clear that he is motivated chiefly by the desire for personal achievement, he is condemned. This problem is not realised in the earlier play; Nungesser represents a change in Brecht's attitude to its values which appears once more in the alterations on which he insisted when it was revived in 1949.

The relationship between the two plays is made clear by the notes to *Der Flug der Lindberghs,* which serve as a kind of "abstract" of the criticism which the earlier "Lehrstück" is to be exposed to in the latter and, in many ways, as an exposition of the actual theme of the *Badener Lehrstück* itself:

> Diese Übung dient der Disziplinierung, welche die Grundlage der Freiheit ist. Der einzelne aber wird zwar nach einem Genußmittel von selber greifen, nicht aber nach einem Lehrgegenstand, der ihm weder Verdienst noch gesellschaftliche Vorteile verspricht. Solche Übungen nützen dem einzelnen nur, indem sie dem Staat nützen, und sie nützen nur einem Staat, der allen gleichmäßig nützen will.[44]

The "State" which the new "Lehrstück" is to serve is no longer a vaguely Utopian technological paradise, it is the socialist state of the future, "der allen gleichmäßig nützen will." The discipline which is the "basis of freedom" is no longer merely a by-product of correct performance, a formal feature, it has become the subject of the work itself as the problem of "Einverständnis." At the same time, Brecht defines clearly and sharply in these notes the function of a work of art which is no longer "Genußmittel" but "Lehrgegenstand" in terms which are in marked contrast to those of the later *Kleines Organon für das Theater.* The separation between "Genuß" and "Nutzen" is complete. The work of art becomes an "Übung" designed to serve the "true" state and to play its part in attaining the "discipline" this state requires.

Nevertheless, and surprisingly enough, it is precisely the "negative aspect" of the *Badener Lehrstück* which remains most remarkable, that which it destroys rather than that which it constructs. The lesson of "Einverständnis" is one which is felt on two levels: the level of the work itself and the level of its "message." For both it means the readiness to accept the almost total destruction of self in order to survive as a part of the new collective, the "true state" — the work of art reduces itself to an "Übung," the individual surrenders name, personality, achievement, life, in order to "return to life" only as a part of the collective, the "gelernter Chor," those who can use his abilities and themselves be of use to him.

44   *Versuche 1—4,* p. 24

It seems hardly a coincidence that in the first speech of the *Lehrstück* (which we have seen to be taken over from *Der Flug der Lindberghs*), the airmen tell us how they have flown "mit einer Schnelligkeit, die den Hurrikan / Um das Doppelte übertraf." In *Mahagonny* Brecht had arrived at the conclusion that "wir brauchen keinen Hurrikan" because man himself is more terrible; in *Der Flug der Lindberghs* man has "beaten" the hurricane again, but in the name of "progress." Coming as it does at the end of the earlier play, this passage carries its full weight of optimism; but with the transposition to the beginning of the *Badener Lehrstück*, its effect becomes markedly different — the lines remain open, for good or bad. The optimism of *Der Flug der Lindberghs* is to be confronted with the findings of *Mahagonny*, and the "storm" which then appears will in many ways remind us of the "hurricane become human" of *Mahagonny*.

The "heroism" of flying is subjected to a severe test in the *Lehrstück:* its use and subservience to the collective. Paul Ackermann's "Gesetz der menschlichen Glückseligkeit" meant, as we have seen, the destruction of any collective, good or bad, because the communal anarchy which it advocated became an anarchy of individual lust for gratification. Here, the "new law" of flying is to be first tested for its "direction," for its positive use to the society which has invented it. The "self-realisation" of the beginning of the play ("Zu der Zeit, wo die Menschheit / Anfing, sich zu erkennen . . .") is a different realisation of self from Paul's, it is the discovery, not of the anarchy of society, but of the means of survival. Flying becomes not a triumph in itself, a victory over the "primitive," as in *Der Flug der Lindberghs,* but a symbol of the possibility of real progress:

> Aufzeigend das Mögliche
> Ohne uns vergessen zu machen: das
> Noch nicht Erreichte.

The collective, in fact, immediately asserts its control over the actions of the individuals:

> Fliegt jetzt nicht mehr.
> Ihr braucht nicht mehr geschwinder zu werden.[45]

The interruption of the action stands for the power of the collective to determine the individual development — it takes over this function in the work of art itself. Like an inquisition, it summons the four airmen to appear before it; symbolically, the plane crashes. In the answering speech of the airmen, Brecht rejects the naive belief in progress:

45 GW 2, p. 590

> ... über dem geschwinderen Aufbruch
> Vergaßen wir unseres Aufbruchs Ziel.[46]

In the preoccupation with "progress" the idea of direction has been lost; this preoccupation has become a "Fieber," a sickness. The airmen are suddenly obliged to "identify" themselves, to justify their survival, and their request for help is to be understood as an admission of dependence on the collective they have "forgotten."

This request for help is first countered by the argument that only those who have "helped" others, who have themselves served the interests of the collective, can expect help of it in return. The natural response of the "crowd" is to provide this help (in the later work this would be termed "die Verführung zur Güte"), but to the question "Haben sie euch geholfen? " they are obliged to answer "Nein." This "Fieber des Städtebaus und des Öls" has not sprung from a desire to "help" humanity, but has grown an end in itself — a criticism which looks forward to the analysis of the development of "science" in Leben des Galilei.

There follows an exposition of the more general problem "Ob der Mensch dem Menschen hilft," a question which Brecht has often answered in his early work, most violently in Die Dreigroschenoper:

> Denn wovon lebt der Mensch? Indem er stündlich
> Den Menschen peinigt, auszieht, anfällt, abwürgt und frißt . . .[47]

The conviction that it is impossible "gut zu sein und doch zu leben," as he expresses it in Der gute Mensch von Sezuan ten years later, remains in Brecht's work to the very end. In order to survive, it is necessary to wrong others. Nevertheless, there is a decisive change between the world of Die Dreigroschenoper and the world of the Badener Lehrstück — in the former, it is up to the individual to assert himself, to fight his way through, to realise the "laws of human happiness" like Paul; here, it is the good of the collective that is important.

This "exposition" is carried out with a clinical exactness, in three "Untersuchungen." In the first, it is demonstrated that the progress of the last four hundred years (since Galileo?) has not relieved "das Elend der Massen" — "Das Brot wurde dadurch nicht billiger." Science has not placed itself in the service of society, but has become a self-sufficient "mechanism." The second demonstration shows projections of the atrocities of war, which Brecht had had opportunity enough to observe in Augsburg towards the end of the First World War. The third is a grotesque clown-number, which anticipates many of the

46 GW 2, p. 591
47 GW 2, p. 458

techniques of the "Theatre of the Absurd." Herr Schmitt, a giant clown, is "not feeling well" — he seems to be in Paul's state of "aber etwas fehlt," but unfortunately for him, he adds to this restlessness the guilelessness of a Galy Gay. His "friends" Einser and Zweier, not villains but "ordinary men," help him to "forget"; like Galy, he is unable to say no. The scene is extraordinary in its systematic brutality, its wholesale sawing-off of limbs. Herr Schmitt, the "simple man," for whom something is "wrong" with the world, is "demontiert" by his well-meaning "friends." ("Denn gerade so ist der Mensch: / Er muß zerstören, was da ist"). He is tortured by his surroundings in the same way as the protagonists of Beckett's mimes, except that the torture is carried out not by abstract powers, but by humans. In the end his limbless rump is left lying on a stone, symbol of the eternal "wrongness" of the world. Schmitt has attained his "kleinste Größe" in a very literal sense indeed; like Galy, he has been systematically stripped of himself by a "bad collective." But it is no longer this bad collective which is to have the last word. When Brecht produced *Mann ist Mann* in 1931, as we have seen, he omitted Galy's "Wachstum ins Verbrecherische"; in the *Badener Lehrstück*, there is a similar turning to the idea of the "right" collective, which is finally to determine whether the Schmitts and Galy Gays shall survive and serve it.

The relationship of this clown-scene to the whole play is important. Schmitt must be brought to realise what "help" he can expect from his fellow-men and revise his behaviour accordingly. He must change his complaint that "something seems to be wrong with the world" and his expectation that help from others will solve the problem into a conscious attempt to change the world. Yet at the same time, he must avoid the solution of Nungesser, who is "heroic," "self-conscious," unable to place the good of the collective above his own good. Nungesser, as we shall see, is in many ways a survival of the anarchical solution of *Mahagonny*, where the individual fights against a hostile society in order to seize as much for himself as possible. Between these two paths lies the way of the "Monteure," who are both less "helpless" and less "self-conscious," who achieve a kind of survival by placing themselves and their "identities" at the service of this new collective, to dispose of as it pleases. The clown-scene provides the proof that "der Mensch hilft dem Menschen nicht" in a most archetypal way, but also the proof that "help" is impossible and inadequate in a society which is based on "Gewalt," and that consequently it is foolish to expect it. Herr Schmitt has yet to realise that "Hilfe und Gewalt geben ein Ganzes / Und das Ganze muß verändert werden." He must learn "der grausamen / Wirklichkeit / Grausamer zu begegnen und / Mit dem Zustand, der den Anspruch erzeugt / Aufzugeben den Anspruch."[48] In this scene of "Hilfeverweigerung," the crowd is brought to see that the answer to the "Gewalt" which already Paul

48 GW 2, p. 599

had found to be, in Adorno's words, "Grund der gegenwärtigen Ordnung," is not "help" but a "Gegengewalt" which strives to establish a new, just order. In Brecht's world, from *Baal* to the last poems, it is the "Gewaltlosen" who are doomed to bear the brunt, and if they survive, it is only by chance.

This is the first statement of a theme which remains central in Brecht's later work. *Johanna, Die Maßnahme* and *Die Ausnahme und die Regel* mark his particular preoccupation with it in this period. The "Gewalt" which we have seen to be at the basis of the city of Mahagonny comes into the open and must be opposed by a new force, the necessity to change the world, even if it too involves the use of "Gewalt." "Hilfe" is rejected because it serves only to maintain the present situation instead of attempting to change it, because it "sugars the pill," and not merely, as in *Mahagonny,* because it brings about the ruin of the individual who allows himself to be "seduced" into it. Individual survival can now be justified only in terms of the good of the collective, in terms of "Einverständnis."

Again, there is an unexpected "continuity" from the earlier work. The rejection of "Hilfe" in these first Marxist plays often seems oddly related to the fear of self-exposure, of sentimentality, which is so characteristic of the early poetry. The balance between sentimentality and scepticism in Brecht's early work is often very delicate indeed; the "Bedrohung" he recognises in his tendency to "sympathise" is countered by an intentional callousness which often reveals more than it conceals. The reluctance to "help" seems also to spring in part from an intellectual consciousness of the dangers of sentimentality for his artistic personality, a fear of "Kitsch" which remains one of the mainsprings of his work. Like Stendhal, he prefers to retreat into the cool perspective of "Vernunft" and to deny his own sensibility by distancing himself from it. The condemnation of the "junger Genosse" in *Die Maßnahme,* for instance, reads at times dangerously like a self-justification for inaction, a convenient proof that what for Brecht is impossible is also "wrong." The arguments presented arrive, to say the very least, at conclusions which are convenient for the inhibitions of the younger Brecht. The "danger" of "Hilfe" in the early work is clear enough – it is an identification with the sufferer, a pity which "exposes" the pitier himself. Like Rilke's Malte Laurids Brigge, he feels threatened by the sufferings of others, which become his own through an excess of "neutrality," they invade his own "blankness."

Brecht's attitude to "Gewalt" in these plays is similarly ambivalent. At this stage, the advocacy of "force against force" has a severity which seems to spring from his new desire to escape from the world of the victims, the Galy Gays and the Schmitts, with whom, nevertheless, he has so much secret sympathy. The harshness with which "goodness" is treated in this early "Lehrstück" has an *ad hominem* quality about it which often tends to make it seem excessive and overstated. The death-wish of the early Brecht, under the threat of the imminent

collapse of self and world which we have seen in *Mahagonny*, gives way to a fear
of death which grows increasingly stronger in the later work, a desire to survive
at any price, which turns him and his principal characters into a set of Schweijks
who make "Gewalt" and death meaningless by their strategy; the "Verweige-
rung" of spontaneous help, the need for political action rather than individual
initiative, which Brecht advocates so strongly at this time, seems often (against
his intention, no doubt) part of this strategy. The progression towards the
"Nichts" which we have analysed in the early work tends here to become a
strange kind of ruse — Brecht attempts to escape by having no "face," by
presenting no surface for attack, by becoming part of the "Nichts" himself. We
shall see just how problematical this survival becomes later, and how in *Leben
des Galilei* Brecht came to revise many of the more extreme aspects of his earlier
"strategy." Here, it often seems that the political argument is secondary to the
individual motivation.

In the "Beratung" which follows, it becomes apparent for the first time that
there is to be a "division" among the four airmen — confronted with the
prospect of death, Nungesser, the pilot, will react differently from the three
"Monteure," who already at this stage indicate their "Einverständnis" with the
idea of death:

> Wir wissen, daß wir sterben werden, aber
> Weißt du es?
> Höre also:
> Du stirbst unbedingt.
> Dein Leben wird dir entrissen
> Du stirbst für dich.
> Es wird dir nicht zugesehen
> Du stirbst endlich
> Und so müssen wir auch.[49]

This is a radical inversion of the "primus inter pares" position we have seen in
Mahagonny and the early work. Nungesser, the "hero" (and his relation to the
early heroes becomes plain in his speech at the end of Scene 8), is now not the
first, but the last of the group of four; it is he who by his "Ichsucht" (compare
Fatzer, "der ichsüchtige") will fail to attain "Einverständnis" and be "driven
out." It is now the three that are right and the one that is wrong. This might
also, of course, be seen as a consequence of *Mahagonny*, where Paul's total
rebellion had ended only in total disillusionment and death.

The "Betrachtung der Toten" of Scene 6 is typical in its starkness and
effectiveness of Brecht's dramaturgy at this stage. The projections give a
"real" quality to the ritual killing of the airmen which is about to begin. The

---

49 GW 2, p. 600

"coldness" with which this demonstration is carried out is in no sense dispassionate; rather is the reverse the case. At this stage, Brecht presents "reality" directly – the "face" of death becomes a nodal point of the play in the consciousness of the audience, and the often obscure action which follows is given a concrete basis. It seems curious, at first, that death, having been presented so directly here, should be explicitly avoided at the end of the play, even for Nungesser, who merely "goes away," but we have already seen how typical this "anticipation" of death is in the early work – in the *Sonett über schlechtes Leben,* for instance, the anticipatory consciousness of death is so complete that nothing further can be added to it during the "short time, which passes so slowly" which follows. Here the reality of death becomes a beginning, rather than an end, as the realisation of the inevitability of death which must precede the attempt to "survive" death by taking its own shape, by extinguishing the "individual" and surviving in the mass, as "no-one."

The "reading of the texts" which follows makes the metaphysical character of the "decision" which is to be reached clear. As we have seen, they form not only the core of the play, but the beginning of a whole new style and form in the later Brecht. The "Sprecher" is Herr Keuner himself, who is prepared to instruct others in the strategy of becoming no-one. The four texts describe this process with an extraordinary relentlessness which reminds us, rather disconcertingly, of the "thoroughness" with which Herr Schmitt was stripped of his members. Text I is a farewell to all sensation, all experience, in so far as it remains individual experience, in that to experience in this way is to remain identifiable and thus exposed. Not only "positive" experience is rejected, but even "negative" experience – not having belongs to, is potentially having. We have seen how the early Brecht, like Malte, was "threatened" by the experience of the external world. In this text, experience is discarded as an initial stage in the attainment of the "kleinste Größe" which is described more fully in Text 2. Yet again, this "giving up" becomes an almost Rilkean "Armut" in its approach to the "Nichts, das denkt" of *Malte.*

The second text remains one of Brecht's most important single utterances about the problem of survival and about his own personal solution to it. The imagery which he chooses to convey this "Gleichnis" is remarkable in its relation to themes and images of the early work. The "storm" of *Mahagonny,* the destructive anarchy of nature and man which we have seen to be the "end" of the "Selbstvernichtungsprozeß," reappears here as the crisis which is to be survived. The "kleinste Größe" itself is in many way reminiscent of the kind of return to the "dunkler Erdenschoß" we have seen from *Baal* onwards – it is a return to the earth in the nakedness of birth, a ritual surrender to death which cheats him of his object. For now, as never before, survival is stated as an established fact: "In seiner kleinsten Größe überstand er den Sturm." With these words the "Sprecher" begs the question of the airmen rather than answering it –

for us, the unanswered question becomes all important: Did "der Denkende" in
fact survive the storm? Did the storm ever subside? Was he in fact ever able to
become "small" enough to escape its batterings? The limitations of the image,
which in the earlier work would scarcely have been obliged to bear the weight of
this conclusion, become apparent. What kind of a "storm" is being described? Is
there any reason to belive that such a storm ever could subside? If not, is there
any value in reducing oneself to one's "kleinste Größe" for the rest of one's
life?

Here, again, there is ambivalence rather than dialectic. True as Brecht's
"Gleichnis" may be if we apply it to a "class," it becomes obscure and
questionable on an individual level. The tendency to equate society with nature,
the anarchy of society with the anarchy of nature, which we have observed in
Mahagonny, revenges itself in this argument. Here, surely, Brecht, in representing
the "opposition" to class survival as a "storm," is guilty of the same kind of
fault that he sees in Courage years later — the tendency to accept politics as
"fate."[50] It is surely not true to say that this "storm" (we are in 1929) can be
fought only by surrendering to it, by becoming "unkenntlich" — so we are
driven back to the "personal" level of the image, where the desire to become
"Nichts," to escape into the no-one, seems more strong than the will to
re-emerge. We shall see that this dual aspect of the character of Herr Keuner,
who is at the same time both Brecht and non-Brecht, both an individual and a
class, is one of the most problematical aspects of the later work, and that Klaus
Heinrich's criticism of Herr K.'s strategy, that "gerade das Nichts ist behaftbar"[51] for him, that he never succeeds in becoming no-one, but at the same time,
remains exposed to the storm, which does not subside, finds unexpected support
in the writings of Brecht's very last years. Here, the problem seems virtually
insoluble; "der Denkende" is advocating a solution which seems open to
objections on both levels and which is only too clearly determined by the very
individual factors that Brecht seems to be trying to reject.

The third is a simple exhortation to "die" which makes it quite clear that
"life" too is a "possession" to be given up if the "kleinste Größe" is to be
reached (we might have been forgiven for assuming from Text 2 that "life" was
the only thing that was not to be given up, indeed that the preservation of life
was the purpose of the whole exercise). Again, the ambivalent nature of the
argument is obvious. This "survival" can only have meaning on the level of the
"many," but it is presented in terms of the individual, and this "individual"
quality becomes even more striking in the fourth Text, where the overall image
again betrays its origins in the early work. "Der Denkende," writes Brecht,
survived the storm, "weil er den Sturm kannte und einverstanden war mit dem

50 GW 17, p. 1150
51 cf. Heinrich, op.cit., p. 56

Sturm." On the first level, we may interpret this as a kind of Marxist prognosis that the world must "get worse to get better," although it is again open to the objections raised in our discussion of Text 2 above; on the second level, it becomes very revealing indeed. Brecht knows the storm because he, like Paul Ackermann, has called for it, has evoked it. The anarchy which he has conjured up is let loose on the world and destroys the world (and Paul/Brecht with it) at whose "base" it lies. Yet now Brecht is "einverstanden" in a very different way from the cataclysmic urge to destroy which informs *Mahagonny*, and especially the Jimmy Mahony of the first version; he wishes for destruction in order that the new may emerge, that a "new" self and a new society may spring phoenix-like from the ashes of the old. He is prepared to sacrifice Jimmy/Paul as "guilty," to let the storm absorb his aggression into a cleansing holocaust in the hope that out of the "Leere," out of the "Niemandsein," life may begin anew.

The "Examen" of Scene 8 represents Brecht's most detailed exposition of the "Keuner" strategy. The recurrence of the word "niemand" and its vital significance in the argument is no coincidence. The three "Monteure," in their "Einverständnis," are offered the possibility of surviving as "Keuners," as "Niemande"; Nungesser, who refuses to become "no-one," who lives only for the continuity of his personality, will be destroyed as "nicht einverstanden," as not at one with the "Fluß der Dinge." The "examination" takes the form of five questions, all of which aim at a reduction of the airmen to their "kleinste Größe," their "Niemandsgestalt"; thus Question 1 emphasises the completely relative, unfinished character of their achievement in "flying," Question 2 the irrelevance of "glory," Question 3 applies itself directly to the problem: "Wer seid ihr? ." The required answer is "wir sind niemand," and Questions 4 and 5 also ask for a "niemand" answer: "niemand wartet auf uns" and "niemand stirbt, wenn wir sterben." The "Monteure" are able to "learn," to achieve the right answer; Nungesser refuses to be "stripped" of his personality and achievement.

This argument is so closely related to the "strategy" of Herr K. analysed by Heinrich that it repays some attention. The conclusion "niemand stirbt, wenn ihr sterbt" combines a "metaphorical" proposition with a real one. "Niemand stirbt" means only "etwas Unwichtiges stirbt"; similarly, the earlier premise "ihr seid niemand" does not, and cannot mean "ihr seid keine Menschen," it has again only metaphorical force. But the argument has a second level. We shall see that the ability of the "Monteure" to become "niemand," in however metaphorical a sense, is the chief reason advanced for the summons to them in the last scene to "return to life" and continue their work in the service of the collective. At this level the argument is characterised by all the difficulties which beset Brecht's "Keunergestalt"; it becomes the highly questionable "syllogism"

No-one dies, if you die
If you die, you do not die

This strategy is again a type of "Flucht nach vorn" which seeks to escape the "Nichts" by becoming it, and in this logical "jump" we have the reflection of the difficulties of the "point of origin," of the true "Nullpunkt" we have discussed above. The problem of identity becomes the stumbling-block; Brecht is representing in terms of individuals a theory which seems fully justifiable only in terms of "class" and collective. He fails to present an adequately dialectical relationship between individual and society, to "re-establish" the individual in terms of the new collective, and the "survival" which he represents thus becomes a survival without the attributes of survival, of individuality. His "Monteure" are thus not able, despite their new "Auftrag," to emerge from their "Niemand-sein," because it is the rule of the new collective; in fact, it seems often the "object" of the whole exercise, rather than a means to the end of creating a new individual in a new society.

Nungesser is unable to become "niemand," not because he is "bourgeois" or supports the existing world order, but out of an individualist anarchy not dissimilar to Paul's:

> Aber ich habe mit meinem Fliegen
> Meine größte Größe erreicht.
> Wie hoch immer ich flog, höher flog
> Niemand.
> Ich wurde nicht genug gerühmt, ich
> Kann nicht genug gerühmt werden
> Ich bin für nichts und niemand geflogen.
> Niemand wartet auf mich, ich
> Fliege nicht zu euch hin, ich
> Fliege von euch weg, ich
> Werde nie sterben.[52]

There is a remarkable blend of irony and sympathy in this passage. Nungesser is "fixed" most clearly by the three heavily accented final "ichs" of the last few lines, and the relativity of his "größte Größe" is emphasised by the ambiguous "niemand" of line 4. "Niemand," the class of "no-ones," will supersede Nungesser's achievements, he has in a very definite sense flown for "nichts und niemand," for nothing, pointlessly, but at the same time also for that class which alone can intergrate his "flying" into its overall progress, whether he will or not. Yet at the same time, we sense a sympathy for him which is developed further in the scene "Die Austreibung" — despite everything, Nungesser is "einer von uns," he is no class enemy, but like the early heroes, is involved in a process from which there is no escape, which prevents him from attaining the "Niemands-gestalt" and surviving in the "Fluß der Dinge." There is a curious reminiscence

52 GW 2, p. 606

of the duet of Paul and Jenny in *Mahagonny* — like the cranes, Nungesser flies "nirgendhin," but somehow bound by the direction of this flight "ins Nichts." Like Paul, he values survival less than the ultimate self-realisation of "Du darfst es." But now his "franchise," the tolerance which society has extended to this purely "individual" activity, is suddenly withdrawn. In the following scene, "Ruhm und Enteignung," he "disappears" when the collective demands the return of the plane (symbol of the collective effort which has gone into his achievement); he is rejected by the "Fluß der Dinge" of which he had been an unconscious part.

The fact that the "alternatives" of *Das Badener Lehrstück* are not so much communism/capitalism as communism/individualism was of course a source of some misunderstanding and criticism on the part of the German Communist Party,[53] which was both somewhat afraid of the starkness with which the communist collective was presented and somewhat irritated by what it regarded as a "bourgeois intellectual" approach to the problem. Yet its importance in Brecht's own development is clear. In the *Badener Lehrstück,* he achieves an "escape" from the all-too-consistent system of the early work which, for all its metaphorical quality, serves as the "jump" for which he had been looking. In a sense, then, we could say that the rejection of Nungesser represents an even more absolute "execution" of the early Brecht than Paul Ackermann's death in *Mahagonny,* and that the "death" of the *Badener Lehrstück* can be taken as the true "midpoint" of Brecht's work, however remarkable it may be that the idea of "personality" should seem to get lost in the process and take years to return.

Nungesser fails, then, to integrate himself into the collective of true progress; his function is taken from him, and with it his "face":

> Dieser
> Inhaber eines Amts
> Wenn auch angemaßt
> Entriß uns, was er brauchte, und
> Verweigerte uns, dessen wir bedurften.
> Also sein Gesicht
> Verlosch mit seinem Amt:
> Er hatte nur eines![54]

His "anarchy" has at last been condemned by the "many faces" of the collective, whom it can only harm. His individualism, for all its achievements, is in the last resort an endangerment of this collective and an exploitation of it — and so the "Amt" which he had held is withdrawn from him. He is a fallen Lindbergh, an "apostle of progress" who has been left behind by the truth

---

53 cf. Schuhmacher, op.cit., pp. 350ff.
54 GW 2, p. 608

Brecht had found in the *Anmerkungen* to *Mahagonny:* that "Wirklicher
Fortschritt ist, was Fortschreiten ermöglicht oder erzwingt."[55] In Nungesser
Brecht rejects the way of Baal and Paul Ackermann, and turns rather to the
Protean, Galy Gay-like quality of the "Monteure," who survive the storm in
their "kleinste Größe." Nungesser's "Austreibung" is remarkable for its elegiac
quality and its echoes of the "Sonett über schlechtes Leben":

> Er ist gezeichnet über Nacht, und
> Seit heute morgen ist sein Atem faulig.
> Seine Gestalt verfällt, sein Gesicht
> Einst uns vertraut, wird schon unbekannt.[56]

He leaves the "stage," is sent out into an empty "Nichts" of waiting and not
being.

In the final scene, "Das Einverständnis," the "return to life" takes place; the
three "Monteure" are ordered to resume their place with a new loyalty to the
collective and placed at the beginning of an infinite dialectic of "Veränderung":

> Zu verändern nicht nur
> Ein Gesetz der Erde, sondern
> Das Grundgesetz.

Nowhere is the infinite nature of this new dialectic of Brecht's clearer than in
this scene, where the airmen are instructed to "give up" each successive stage of
progress to work for the next:

> Habt ihr die Welt verbessert, so
> Verbessert die verbesserte Welt.
> Gebt sie auf!
> . . . .
> Habt ihr die Welt verbessernd die Wahrheit vervollständigt, so
> Vervollständigt die vervollständigte Wahrheit.
> Gebt sie auf!
> . . . .
> Habt ihr die Wahrheit vervollständigend die Menschheit verändert, so
> Verändert die veränderte Menschheit.
> Gebt sie auf!
> . . . .
> Ändernd die Welt, verändert euch!
> Gebt euch auf![56]

The "giving up of the self," the "Nullpunkt" of the Lehrstück, is elevated to a
necessary condition of this "Veränderung," as part of the readiness to give up

55 GW 2, p. 609
56 GW 2, p. 611–12

"completeness" in favour of true progress. Indeed, we could see *Mahagonny* — and the Brecht of Mahagonny — as "completed truths" of this kind which must be given up in order to be "completed" further. Yet the "truth" could not be said to progress by becoming "nothing"; it arises out of the truth" that went before it in a dialectical process, and retains in itself the "truth" of that first "truth." Logically then, the "truths" of the early Brecht should be subsumed in these new truths, and not merely superseded. This is, however, precisely what Brecht seems to wish to avoid at this stage — the early Brecht must be reduced to zero and his ideas rejected, like Nungesser's. It is only much later, in *Bei Durchsicht meiner ersten Stücke,* that he attempts to demonstrate such a process in the development of his early work, and even then, he is less than fair to its "Wahrheitsgehalt." The problem remains, that the "conversion" of the late twenties forms for Brecht's own consciousness less a decisive point in the organic development of his work than a "new beginning," and the "loss of identity" which this self-rejection brings with it seems to dog his work for a number of years after. Just as Herr K. is unable truly to become "no-one," so Brecht is unable to dismiss the consequences of his own early period; he too remains "recognisable." The "new start," as in *Leben des Galilei* years later, runs the risk of being revealed rather as the "bitter end." By denying the continuity in his own development, by attempting to trivialise and conceal the experiential truth of his earlier work, Brecht does himself a disservice, in that he is also trivialising his own motivation. A synthesis between old and new seems to be required, and I hope to show that it was this that Brecht was in fact attempting in his late works.

To sum up, then, in the *Badener Lehrstück* we have Brecht's own direct representation of the "crisis" through which he has passed in these years and his plan for survival. His adoption of a "positive dialectic" seems, however, to come into some conflict with the rather undialectic quality of his attempt to save his individuality by losing it. The result is an extreme personal reticence coupled with a marked "loss of identity" in the works themselves. The characters in his plays are stripped of their own individuality because it has no place in his concern to lose his own. In *Das Badener Lehrstück,* as in *Die Maßnahme* and *Der Jasager,* Brecht fails to achieve a new dialectic of individual and society. The collective becomes a characterless "wir" from which the individual has been driven out as aggressive and anarchical, instead of itself a "collective of individuals." Brecht seems on the one hand to be trying to force the progression of his early work to an end, in order to "continue," but on the other, he seems unable to escape from this "end-state." What emerges on the "other side" lacks "life" — since life produces individuals as surely as classes or collectives. The identity which has been lost from Brecht's work must somehow be reinvested, if it is to regain its former expansion.

IV

darin aber ist der böse baal der asoziale groß
daß seine stimme durch ben bericht seines feindes
der ihn beschreibt die meine
hindurchdringt
mich bezichtigend ich hätte
von heiterkeit erfüllt
so lange er die ausbeuter ausbeutete
und die verwerter verwertete
ihn schlechter behandelt
als er auch meiner gesetzte spottete
aber dies ist seine schuld
darum ist er der asoziale geheißen
daß an ihn billige forderungen stellend
der vollkommene staat wie ein ausbeuter dastünde.[57]

Der böse Baal der asoziale

How dominant the Baal/Keuner confrontation was in Brecht's thinking at this time can most clearly be seen in his plan to include such a confrontation in a series of small *Lehrstücke* under the title *Der böse Baal der asoziale,* which he still hoped to complete as late as 1938, and which have only recently been published in fragmentary form by Dieter Schmidt. It was not the first time Brecht had attempted to "revise" his first play in the light of the new insights of the late twenties; already in 1926 he had produced a version entitled *Lebenslauf des Mannes Baal*[58] which, as Alfred Kerr remarked, clearly showed his desire to "distance it from himself." The (almost certainly fictive) biographical sketch "Das Urbild Baals,"[59] also dates from this phase; it is an obvious attempt on Brecht's part to destroy the identification which had marked all the early versions and turn the play into an objective "dramatische Biographie." The few fragments of *Der böse Baal der asoziale* which remain, however, are perhaps even more significant, for all their sketchiness, in that the Baal figure is now not only directly criticised, but is opposed by Brecht's new *alter ego,* Keuner. Again, the figure of Keuner is introduced only in the "zweite Schicht"; as in *Fatzer,* the critical balance finally demands the introduction of a "positive" character who will exemplify the insights gained from the criticism of the "Baal" figure. It is significant, too, that Brecht never succeeded in completing either project; in fact, in the verses quoted at the beginning of this section, he is disarmingly frank

---

57 *Baal. Der böse Baal der asoziale,* ed. D. Schmidt, Frankfurt 1968, (abbreviated: BBDA), p. 90
58 Now published in *Baal. Drei Fassungen,* Frankfurt 1966.
59 BBDA, p. 103

about the problems involved. For all the severe logic of Fatzer's condemnation, he continues to dominate the play; so, too, does the voice of Baal penetrate the "bericht seines feindes," the new Brecht, touching him, in fact, on his sorest spot: he "makes fun" of the new laws which Brecht has discovered — even the perfect state, since it too must curtail his individuality and put his talents to use, would seem an "exploiter" to him. Baal shares with Fatzer an "ichsüchtiges Wesen" which rejects all attempts at "Verwertung"; curiously, although the author's "philosophical" sympathy has been withdrawn, he still remains fascinated by their total rebellion, even after having proved so many times, from *Mahagonny* onwards, that it can only bring about their own destruction and that of the world about them. Brecht's commitment to the apocalyptic dies hard.

Baal's answer to the question "wie ihm der gang der dinge gefallen habe" — "ausgezeichnet,"[60] is a repetition of Jimmy Mahony's farewell speech in the first version of *Mahagonny;* he does not wish to change the system, but to play it on its own terms. The central problem of the "Fragment" is in fact the problem of "Verwertung": Baal refuses to be "verwertet" by anyone or anything, just as he would refuse to be used even by the "perfect state." Yet Brecht comes to the conclusion that Baal himself is a "Verwerter"; in B 6.17[61] he writes "der böse Baal, d. asoziale, verwertet lyrik, um sich einen Menschen dienstbar zu machen," and in B 6.23 he defines his position even more clearly:

> im ersten abschnitt tritt baal unter den verwertern auf. obwohl baal selber ein verwerter ist kann er sich mit diesen leuten nicht einigen da seine art zu groß ist. der kleinen art entsprechend herrscht unter ihnen eine gewisse niedrige ordnung welche sie verwerten. baal durch die offene und wilde art seines ichsüchtigen wesens macht sie sich zu erbitterten feinden. seine art ist eine geistige und also höher stehende da sie in der form dem inhalt entspricht indem das auftreten des bösen baal des asozialen so gewalttätig ist wie seine filosofie.

Baal's "große art" is, of course, directly related to the "grosse härte" and "ausserordentliche kühnheit" Brecht had demanded of the heroes of "die neue Zeit" between the Great War and the "Sintflut," and his conflict with the "verwerter" is only a further echo of Jimmy Mahony's conflict with the powers of *Mahagonny.* Just as Jim destroys the façade of "Ruhe und Eintracht" which Begbick has set up to protect her interests and exposes the essential violence on which the whole system is based, so Baal too practises "Verwertung" in its extreme, anarchical form; the appeal of his strategy lies in its consistency — there

---

60 BBDA, p. 78
61 The numbering is Schmidt's (*BBDA*, pp. 78—90). B 6 = "Szenen, Entwürfe, Fragmente" No. 6; the fragments of *BBDA* are grouped under this heading and numbered consecutively from 1—26. It is a pity Schmidt does not simply give the Archiv numbers, but I have chosen to retain his system for the sake of convenience.

is no disagreement between "form" and "content," his behaviour gives direct
expression to the philosophical insight that the society which surrounds him is
equally "asozial" and "gewalttätig" beneath the mask of its "niedrige ordnung."

Keuner, however, "uses" people not for himself but for the state (B 6.24).
B 6.13 shows succinctly the common ground he shares with Baal, while at the
same time stressing his overriding preoccupation with the good of the collective.
After listening to the "Choral vom bösen Baal," an "Arbeiter" protests: "die
wörter sind gut aber der inhalt hat keinen wert für den staat." Baal and Keuner
unanimously reject this distinction between "form" and "content" ("die wörter
sind der inhalt") — to divide "form" and "content" is itself a form of
"Verwertung" typical of a "schlechter Staat" — yet Keuner continues, to claim
that the "good" state *can* make use of Baal's poetry, and that to judge a man,
"nach dem was er abliefert" is typical of a bad state. This is a particularly subtle
distinction: Keuner's ideal state can make use of people and things, but it does
not degrade the person by judging him only as "producer," which is, in effect, a
form of "Entfremdung." Put simply, his argument (supported elsewhere in the
fragment) might read: the things are there for the people, not the people for the
things. Baal, however, "die nicht eßbare Pflaume"[62] (cf. the "Fuhrleute" in the
"Branntweinschenke" scene of the final version: "Pflaumen soll sie fressen!"[63])
refuses to be "verwertet" altogether, rejecting even the "billige forderungen" of
the perfect state. As such, he must be rejected; the original sympathy (B 6.24) of
the audience, which the author clearly shares, must be changed to antipathy, and
like Fatzer, he must be "ausgemerzt."

Two of the fragmentary scenes, taken together, cast a surprising light on the
genesis of the *Keunergeschichten*. B 6.12 is clearly a prototype of the later
Keuner anecdote "Gastfreundschaft,"[64] though there is an important change in
perspective. Herr Keuner, who has invited Baal, refuses to select guests "die zu
ihm passen," or to prepare a special meal for him and tells the "Freundin"
(Baal's?) to put on a "hübsches kleid" "ohne gründe," not from any feeling of
obligation. He believes that "bei jeder gelegenheit ist es gut jenes bild
herzustellen das der art nach der welt entspricht." In the later version, Herr K.
adopts this strategy as guest, he does not alter in any way the room he has been
given, but seeks rather to adjust himself to his new surroundings; as host,
however, he "adjusts" himself to his guest by re-arranging the furniture slightly,
but with the typical comment "Und es ist besser, ich entscheide, was zu ihm
paßt!." These two "Haltungen," of course, complete one another, together they
are a typical example of Herr K.'s "Höflichkeit"; the one attitude demands the
other. In *Der böse Baal der asoziale*, however, Baal is more than a match for

62   BBDA, p. 83
63   BBDA, p. 24
64   GW 12, p. 386

Herr K.'s politeness, as can be seen from B 6.11; Baal's severe conclusion that "schlechtes essen" is better than "sympathie" is realistic, but denies, in its asocial logic, the whole concept of a state based on "Gemeinnutz" which is at the basis of Keuner's attitude. The later version thus virtually implies the "exclusion" of the "Baal" type in order to sustain its polite dialectical balance.

B 6.21, on the other hand, gives us a curious example of an act of Baal's being transferred in the *Keunergeschichten* to K. himself. The anecdote "Der hilflose Knabe"[65] is identical in all details, except that Baal has been replaced by Keuner as the "teacher" who shows the boy "der gewöhnliche ausgang aller appelle der schwachen." Here again, an interesting development in perspective has taken place. Baal's aim is, like Keuner's, in a sense pedagogical, but it is a destructive pedagogy which suits well with his characterisation; the lesson that his "Schüler" Lupu is to draw from this encounter is the validity of Baal's asocial "Stärke," the recognition of the law of the jungle on which society is based. In the context of the *Keunergeschichten,* however, the parable has a quite different effect, as we shall see; it is only one aspect of a discussion of the problem of protest and survival, and Herr K.'s actions appear "educative" in a different sense (significantly, the "Schüler" has disappeared); the boy must learn the consequences of ineffective protest. K. has simply adopted the role of Baal, the asocial, for pedagogical purposes.

It is, of course, scarcely surprising that the extremity of opposition between Baal/Fatzer and Keuner should later give way to a more conciliatory attempt to unite the two, yet the severity of the rejection itself makes such a reconciliation difficult. The fragment *Der böse Baal der asoziale* has a particular importance in an understanding of this process, if only because it is the one work in which Brecht directly identifies the two poles of the argument he was conducting in these years with his earlier self.

V

Ein Mann, der Herrn K. lange nicht gesehen hatte, begrüßte ihn mit den Worten: "Sie haben sich gar nicht verändert." "Oh!" sagte Herr K. und erbleichte.

Geschichten vom Herrn Keuner[66]

65 GW 12, p. 381
66 GW 12, p. 383

As Brecht continues to utilise the figure of Herr Keuner, it becomes
increasingly clear that not only has the "storm" failed to abate, but that he has
after all been unable to achieve his "kleinste Größe," so much so, that critic
after critic[67] has seen in this "No Man" an "idealised self-portrait" of Brecht
himself. Nor is he unaware of this danger — in the anecdote "Das Wiedersehen"
Herr K. grows "deathly pale" when a friend recognises him and tells him that he
"hasn't changed a bit".[68] As Heinrich writes, "er ist ertappt als Nicht-Keuner,"
recognised for what he is, and has thus failed to "escape" from the storm which
threatens him. The "flight into the goal" has been after all only a metaphor, a
ruse, and the situation which Brecht has described in the *Sonett über schlechtes
Leben* has not really changed; Herr Keuner attempts to anticipate the "end" of
his existence, the "Nichts" to which he must inevitably be reduced, but is left
waiting all too recognisably for this "reluctant end" (a species of Godot) to
arrive. The attempt to "overtake" this projected end, instead of providing him
with a release, marks him more clearly than ever, — to quote Heinrich once
more:

> Die heutigen Niemandsgestalten wollen ein Hohlraum sein: wirklich ein
> Nichts. Aber, wie die Gestalten Robbe Grillets zeigen: der Hohlraum gerade,
> das Negativ, ist behaftbar. — Herr K. hat die Schwierigkeiten des Niemand
> nicht gelöst. Er hat sie erläutert und dadurch sich als Identität kenntlich
> gemacht. Es ist sehr fraglich, ob er schon der "Denkende" war, der "in seiner
> kleinsten Größe" den Sturm übersteht.[69]

The "Sog," the self-destructive whirlpool of the early work remains an
unmistakable factor in the "second optimism" of Herr Keuner, who arrives at a
position remarkably close to the memorable paradox with which Walter
Benjamin concludes his profound essay on Goethes *Wahlverwandtschaften:* "Nur
um der Hoffnungslosen willen ist uns die Hoffnung gegeben."[70] The "optimism"
which hopes for an emergence from the cave, for an abating of the storm, is not
"natural," it can be reached only by a radical "Verfremdung" of the estranged
world about us. As Brecht writes in one of the most direct of his later poems:

> Ich habe gehört: daß die Elenden die Herren von morgen sind
> Das sei das Natürliche. Ein Blick genüge
> Es zu sehen. Das
> Kann ich nicht finden.[71]

67 cf., for example, Konrad Farner, "Über die Weisheit in unserem Zeitalter," *Sinn und
Form*, 2. Sonderheft, p. 115.
68 GW 12, p. 383
69 Heinrich, op.cit., p. 56
70 Walter Benjamin, *Illuminationen*, Frankfurt 1961, p. 147
71 GW 9, p. 752

The implied "nevertheless" of this poem is the hope which animates Herr Keuner in his perpetual difficulties in the disguise of "No Man:" that, as in the aphorism "Irrtum und Fortschritt,"[72] the "errors" of the individual, who can never truly rid himself of his individual fallibility, may be "carried" by the overall upward movement of the historical dialectic with which he declares himself "einverstanden," by the "Fluß der Dinge."

Thus it is only half the truth to see in Herr K. a self-portrait of Brecht, and many of the superficial difficulties of the stories result from the tendency to assume that Herr K. is an "individual" in this way. We have seen how strong was the "rejection of self" which led to his "creation," and even if this rather drastic procedure is subjected later on to a more dialectic development, it is nevertheless clearly an error to see in the later Herr Keuner merely the individual and not "the collective of no-ones" in which he originally found his justification and sole purpose. The real secret of Herr K.'s survival, for all his "special" characteristics, is the fact that he stands as much for a class, which cannot perish, as for an individual, who must. Walter Benjamin wrote of the first version of *Leben des Galilei* that "the people are the hero," for it is they who "carry" Galileo's knowledge and must turn it to their own use; in the same way, Herr Keuner's wisdom, like Laotse's, has its justification only in those who "demand" it of him, who help it into fact. In his "class" role, Herr K. cannot die, he can only return to the "Fluß der Dinge" to emerge in another shape and form and continue, however slowly and painfully, in the same general direction of hope. There is no evidence that for Brecht this hope was ever a hope for "Marx in our time"; his utterances on the subject of the "Utopia" which lies at the end of the road make it clear that for him always "das Ziel lag in großer Ferne." Indeed, the direction seems often more important than the "goal" — his dialectic is in a very real sense infinite, incapable of completion. Herr K.'s "errors" can only be justified if he is "einverstanden" with this direction; as soon as his individual acts become "fertig," complete in themselves, he is doomed.

Yet it is precisely in this "dual" nature of Herr K. that one of the chief dangers of Brecht's strategy seems to lie. The dialectic of individual and class which he incorporates often comes close to being twisted into a false self-justification for individual inaction, i.e., what does it matter what the individual does if the class survives? Many of the *Geschichten* describe courses of action which seem natural, even obvious, on the class level, but, like *Die Maßnahme,* seem to excite our disagreement almost intentionally on the individual level — Brecht's failure to identify himself, to expose himself to attack, runs the risk (which was to materialise years later in the third version of *Leben des Galilei*) of pursuing strategy to the point of betrayal. He seems, at least in the early *Keunergeschichten,* to fail to grasp the full significance of the dialectic argument of Marx, which sees the revolution as at one and the same time the product of scientific necessity, and of the constructively employed "free will" of individuals. Brecht, as the party critics were quick enough to point out in the thirties, seems too inclined to submerge the individual beneath the historical determinism of the overriding dialectic. It is clear that the dialectic can only progress through the acts of individuals who are "einverstanden" with it, and that to remove individuality is more often than not to remove the power to act. The insistence on the "many faces" of the party seems often to forget that these faces are the faces of many individuals.

Again, we may see this ambivalence as the result of a subterranean survival from the early work, of the attempt to "flee into the goal." Herr K. is too aware of the persistence of danger to emerge from the disguise into which he has been driven; he places only too often the strategy of personal survival before the interests of eventual class victory. So long as he can plead the necessity to remain "no-one," to survive so that his "Wissen" may not be lost, he is excused from positive action of the kind that might endanger his life in a real, and not a metaphorical sense. We suspect him of really wishing to become a "nothing" in order to be freed from the necessity of reacting to a world which, from first to last, is an assault on his hope and on his sensitivity. Even as a person, Herr Keuner is divided — on the one hand he represents the Odyssean hero who has "overcome" the storm and death, on the other he himself must cast doubt on this survival by the persistence of his disguise and the ambiguity of his motives.

It is significant that one of the *Keunergeschichten* which deals directly with this problem of survival, the parable "Maßnahme gegen die Gewalt,"[73] should have been included in the first version of the play *Leben des Galilei*, in slightly altered form:[74] the Herr Egge of the original ("Ecke mit weichem 'g,' an dem sich niemand stoßen kann"[75]) becomes the "Cretan philosopher Keunos," just another of Herr K.'s many aliases (he has learnt from the *Badener Lehrstück* the danger of having only one "face"). For the three versions of *Galilei* mark an increasing awareness on Brecht's part of the problematical nature of Herr Keuner's survival — indeed, in the final version, he seems to condemn this strategy as betrayal. The story of Herr Egge, with which Galileo foreshadows his "tactical renunciation" in the first version leaves so many questions unanswered that it was only to be expected that Brecht would return to it in later years. Most of all, Herr Egge's conduct seems to depend for its justification on the "dual nature" of Herr K. we have analysed above. For seven years he submits to the agent who has been given power over him, and only when the latter dies of luxury and laziness does he answer his demand for service with a heartfelt "no!."

---

73 GW 12, p. 375
74 cf. Gerhard Szczesny, *Das Leben des Galilei und der Fall Bertolt Brecht*, Berlin 1966, p. 107
75 Heinrich, op.cit., p. 53

For seven years he becomes a "no-one," gives up his "face" and his purpose in order to survive. Yet, as Klaus Heinrich writes, "Fragen drängen sich auf":

> hätte Herr Egge den Agenten bekehren können? Herr Egge nicht. War es Zufall, daß er am Leben blieb? Es war Zufall. War der stumme Protest wenigstens wirksam? Hat ihn jemand als Protest verstanden? Herr Keuner ja. Wogegen wehren sich diese beiden, Herr Egge und Herr Keuner? — Sie wehren sich, selbst wenn sie Vorträge halten (z.B. gegen die Gewalt), nicht gegen die Gewalt, sondern gegen das Sich-Verstricken durch Sprache. Odysseus, ohne den Ruhm des Überlebens im Gesang, wäre: niemand. Herr Keuner ohne das Hinabsteigen in Namenlosigkeit, Herr Egge ohne das ihn rettende Verstummen, wäre nun erst: niemand. Er wäre jetzt erst wirklich auf dem Niemandsnamen ertappt. Also ist es nur eine Flucht vor dem Niemandsein in das Niemandsein? [76]

Herr Egge's solution, like Galileo's in the first version of the play, remains — problematical. Survival in itself is not enough; Herr Egge's "Wissen," like Galileo's, must reach the class which can give it meaning and translate it into fact. Herr Keuner ist not merely Schweijk, he is Laotse, "der Lehrer Brecht," as well, and, like Laotse, his relation to those for whom his "Lehre" is designed is, to say the least, complex. He cannot apply his wisdom himself, it must be "demanded" of him by the collective. The unity of Schweijk and Laotse is an uneasy one; the "survival" of the early thirties is as much the desire of the "teacher" to survive, even if it means the renouncing of his teachings, as it is a strategy of survival for a whole class. Often it seems to be little more than a ruse designed to save precisely that personality which it claims to eliminate. Yet, after all, Herr Egge (unlike Galy Gay, who lets himself be "seduced" into joining the "evil" collective) has learnt 'to say "no",' as Herr Keuner explicitly informs us, and his realisation that now is not the time to say it may be justified by circumstance.

It is characteristic of the *Keunergeschichten* that "Maßnahmen gegen die Gewalt" is opposed and completed by two other anecdotes, "Das Recht auf Schwäche" and "Der hilflose Knabe."[77] In the latter, the failure of the boy to protest adequately is punished by the passer-by, who is thereby put in a position to take further advantage of his weakness. The boy's second protest is worse than futile; he has not learnt how to say "no," and by protesting at the wrong time and in the wrong way exposes himself completely. Yet Herr Egge is in no position to "shout" his defiance — and even the boy's silence might have saved him only one of his "Groschen," and that, perhaps, only briefly (why did the first thief leave it with him if not to return for it later!?). Similarly, Herr K.'s

76 op.cit., p. 72
77 GW 12, p. 380—1

"right to display human weakness" would scarcely have helped Herr Egge, who is not in a position to protest or complain. This limitation of the situation ("Wer A sagt, der muß nicht B sagen"[78]) is of course typical of Brecht's work, where each situation must be thought out for itself, but it reveals the danger of a false estimation of the circumstances (cf. the Vanni sub-plot in *Galileo III*). The "Wissender" is faced with the ultimate danger that his survival through non-protest may end as betrayal because, like the third Galileo, he has underestimated the strength of his own position and allows his enemies to exploit his silence or his strategic lies for their own purposes. Herr Egge's solution is, after all, dependent on a freak of chance, on a passive and not wholly rational waiting in a situation which may well prove hopeless. Herr Keuner is no "hilfloser Knabe," he is the by-stander, who, in teaching the boy a cruel lesson, is at the same time thinking of his own interests – to survive, he must take advantage of others (like Courage), if he is to endure until a suitable occasion arises for saying the "no" he has learnt to say but seems never to have used. As Heinrich writes: "Erkennen für eine bessere Welt ist eine schöne Aufgabe. Doch Überwintern (Herr K. nannte es noch Überleben) ist häufig die einzige, ungemein anstrengende, die bleibt."[79] In the last resort, Herr K. is left stranded by the failure of the new collective to appear and make his "waiting" meaningful – the "better world" fails to emerge, and Herr K. remains an idealist and a Utopian who is, however, not beyond filling in his time in agreeable ways.

The "Humpfklub" which Brecht describes in "Mißverstanden"[80] has solved the problem of protesting in an even more ingenious way. Robbed of their right to express an opinion, its members meet yearly and after an excellent meal are allowed their one word, "Humpf," to express the untold grievances of the past twelve months. Herr Keuner's sympathy is apparent: ' "Ich hörte allerdings," sagte Herr K. kopfschüttelnd, "daß auch dieses 'Humpf' von einigen mißverstanden wird, indem sie annehmen, das bedeute *nichts.*" ' Like Herr Egge, the members of the "Humpfklub" preserve their self-respect by a "silent protest," one which enables them to endure their "servitude" without forgetting their basic opposition, like the Israelites *super flumina Babylonis*. Here, however, the solution seems even more ironic than in "Maßnahmen gegen die Gewalt": the meal is excellent, the saying of "Humpf" seems to carry in itself the danger of petrifying into a mere ritual, the remains of a weary resignation which no longer really believes that the time will come when it will no longer be necessary to "refrain from expressing an opinion," that they will live to see the good fortune of Herr Egge who survives the rule of "Gewalt" to register his protest with an eventual "No." It is, furthermore, an isolated and "aristocratic" protest – one

---

78 cf. GW 2, p. 629
79 Heinrich, op.cit., p. 55
80 GW 12, p. 398

might almost be forgiven for comparing it with the "protest" of the "Gruppe 47," which often seemed to take the form of "signs" agreed on by members and meaningful only to them. The danger of Herr K.'s club *is* precisely that the "Humpf" may come to mean nothing, that its original purpose may be forgotten or despaired of. It is difficult to resist the temptation to see an analogy with Brecht's own behaviour in East Berlin in this "Humpf," the retreat into the indirect and oblique, which seems often the cover for a deep pessimism. The poem "Böser Morgen" is a critique of Herr Keuner, who is so busy practising his logic of survival that he forgets to communicate his "knowledge" to those who need it:

> Heut nacht im Traum sah ich Finger, auf mich deutend
> Wie auf einen Aussätzigen. Sie waren zerarbeitet und
> Sie waren gebrochen.
> Unwissende! schrie ich
> Schuldbewußt.[81]

Herr Keuner's optimism can exist only in conjunction with a pessimism which is its genesis and justification. The "unsolved questions" of "Überzeugende Fragen"[82] are as essential to his dialectic as the errors of "Mühsal der Besten";[83] the present can only be given meaning, shape, by a "direction" consciously imposed on it by hope in the future. The eventual "goal" here serves the same function that the "Nichts," the end of the self-destructive process, carries out in the early work — it is the sole fixed point, and yet unattainable. The "error" of the present is carried by the "hope" of the future. So long as the present is not "fertig," there is hope, for in its "openness" lies the possibility of development. But those who "work after one" are not susceptible of proof. In the last resort, Brecht is "projecting value into history"[84] as surely as Marx and Hegel, but without the belief in progress of either. For him, this "projection" is fundamentally a moral decision which must often be made against the evidence — it is not Herr K. himself who "kommt weiter," who progresses, but those hoped-for successors of his, who are necessary to "prove" his argument.

Brecht's fear of things becoming "finished" remains constant throughout his life. It is a fear of presenting a fixed surface to the attack, of becoming caught in his own work (where he seems always to have felt that he has no right to be), of "Sich-Verstricken durch Sprache." The members of the "Humpfklub" are all men whose statements are perpetually "misunderstood," and for this reason they impose silence on themselves in the form of the "Humpf." But Brecht remains a "writer," he must continue to speak, to resist the "Sprachlosigkeit,"

---

81   GW 10, p. 1010
82   GW 12, p. 382
83   GW 12, p. 377
84   cf. Hermann Broch, *Die Schlafwandler*, Zürich n.d., p. 594

the speechlessness which Heinrich sees as merely another aspect of the "loss of identity" with which he is threatened, and which is the logical solution to his problem. He does not detach himself from his work, like Kafka from his Odradek, so much as submit it to constant change, exploit the intentional opennesses of his work to shift its meaning and to disappear between them. In a sense, then, it is almost a contradiction in terms to attempt to find *the* meaning, *the* conclusion of one of Brecht's parables, since their essence is to have more than one. On the other hand, the work itself often seems to militate against this "Umfunktionieren," and, like Herr Keuner, to betray itself as the product of a particular situation which cannot easily be transferred at will. Brecht seems often to be doing violence to his own works, demonstrating in effect only that the meaning of the work lies between the interpretations he derives from it. It is, for instance, hard to see *Leben des Galilei* either as the hymn of Keunerian cunning the first version seems to intend, or as the wholesale condemnation of this cunning in the final scene in its 1955 form; the bulk of the play remains, and Galileo remains a difficult character who has bought the right to survive with a strategy which makes his survival of questionable value for the collective. Herr Keuner, however much he appeals to the collective of no-ones for justification, remains Brecht.

So also the elephant of "Herrn K.'s Lieblingstier"[85] is an ambivalent beast, both Brecht and non-Brecht, both "kenntlich" and "unkenntlich." It is the survivor among animals ("it lives to a ripe old age") as K. wishes to remain the survivor among men. The elephant is, after all, not a "collective," it is a single animal, and its proletarian habits have an element of condescension. The elephant survives because he is not ordinary, any more than Brecht is "ordinary"; he is a king of animals turned democrat, an intellectual who disguises himself in proletarian clothing in an attempt to conceal the identity which troubles him: "Er trägt seine Identität als eine Last mit sich herum und kann sie nicht loswerden: sie hat ihn verraten."

Nowhere is the paradoxical quality of Brecht's "eingreifendes Denken" more clear than in the three-legged fowl of "Herr Keuner und die Zeichnung seiner Nichte."[86] The necessary end ("Flying," again a symbol of progress) suggests a means (the extra leg) which is "against nature," for nature itself seems to deny progress. The image is intentionally a refractory one — again, Brecht is close to Benjamin's paradox. Fowls must fly; hopelessness is itself the ground for hope. In the *Keunergeschichten* this extreme of hopelessness is felt most clearly in the impatience with which Brecht longs for the time when it will be possible once more to be "freundlich," to have "Kennzeichen guten Lebens" about one, when "Genuß" will be free from "Schimpfliches" and "Auszeichnendes." The final

85 GW 12, p. 387
86 GW 12, p. 400

problem remains: how is it possible for a new world to emerge after the second of Herr Keuner's "zwei Hergaben? "

> Doch ist von ihm eine weitere Hergabe bekannt, welche schwieriger war. Auf seinem Wege nämlich des Verborgenwerdens kam er für Zeiten wieder in ein größeres Haus, dort gab er, kurz bevor ihn die blutigen Wirren seiner Voraussage nach verschlangen, seine Decke weg für eine reichere oder für viele Decken, und auch den Sack gab er weg, mit einem Satze des Bedauerns und den fünf Sätzen des Einverständnisses, wie er auch seine Weisheit vergaß, damit die Auslöschung vollständig würde. Dies war die schwere Hergabe.[87]

This passage is virtually the "reductio ad absurdum" of Herr Egge's "Verstummen"; the questions which troubled us there are here even more insistent. "Einverständnis" ceases to have a meaning when the collective for whom the "Träger des Wissens" preserves his knowledge is itself cast in doubt. What purpose does this "extinguishment" of Herr K.'s knowledge fulfil? Firstly, we are struck by the fact that it contradicts itself – despite "Auslöschung," Herr K.'s "surrender" is "bekannt"; and because it is "bekannt," he has lost none of those things he has given up, only his life, and we have seen just how ambivalent this "surrender of life" is in our discussion of the *Badener Lehrstück*. It is again the "collective" aspect of Herr K., the indestructible representative of humanity, which rescues him from "extinguishment." (Compare Brecht's statement in the later preface "Bei Durchsicht meiner ersten Stücke": "Es ist unmöglich, das Glücksverlangen der Menschen ganz zu töten."[88]) Again he is exploiting the "niemand stirbt, wenn ihr sterbt" of the *Lehrstück*. The dead live on as part of the community of no-ones who will one day come to rule the world, the wisdom of "der Denkende" remains with his class, who demand of him, as the "gelernter Chor" of the *Lehrstück* demands of the airmen, the "ability to die." He surrenders his "wisdom" in the interest of the dialectic: "Habt ihr die Welt verbessernd die Wahrheit vervollständigt, so / Vervollständigt die vervollständigte Wahrheit. / Gebt sie auf!" Yet we remain troubled by this "survival," even if the "blutige Wirren," the extreme negative phase of the dialectic, are presented as the executioner who removes the suspicion that the "fine house" and the "many blankets" have something to do with the decision. Friedrich Dürrenmatt treats the same problem more convincingly in his early play *Romulus der Große:* Romulus too can only justify his actions, or rather, his failure to act, by an appeal to the imagined executioner who will give his death the character of an atonement and thereby refute the criticisms of laziness, cowardice and self-excuse which are levelled at him by others in the play, but he is to be denied this relief; he is pensioned off to an estate in the Campagna. His sacrifice is

[87] GW 12, p. 406
[88] GW 17, p. 948

neither required nor accepted. In the same way, there seems no need for the
"Denkender" to remain "unkenntlich" at the price of his wisdom when he has
no longer anything to lose but his life. His failure to protest under these
conditions springs from a pessimism which is a betrayal of his knowledge. Herr
Keuner provides too easy a method of survival; we suspect that, with their
pensions and their "blankets" he and Romulus are not so unhappy as they
would have us believe. Romulus, too, conceals his knowledge out of a conviction
that the world is working in his direction: he damns Rome rather than attempt
to save it by changing it. The passivity of both is suspect.

The problem of survival becomes a vital element in the later plays. Herr K.'s
"solution" becomes an almost metaphysical hope whose purpose is to correct
the almost unrelieved pessimism with which life is presented in these works; a
hope that the tragedy of the individual, the "giving up" of all that is valuable in
order to survive, will find its justification in the dialectic of history, which,
working through the "no-ones," will change the world that makes such
"surrenders" necessary. It is not "natural" to see the masters of tomorrow in the
oppressed of today — "nature" must be changed. It is this faith in the possibility
of a change which Brecht requires in his readers if they are to arrive at the
conclusions which he demands of them and yet leaves them to reach on their
own. He can only show us the world as it is and hope that we will come to
believe, with him, not only that it ought to be changed, but that it can be. More
he cannot do. In a play such as *Mutter Courage und ihre Kinder* this
unwillingness to give more than the premises of an argument from which more
than one conclusion can be drawn results in a definite ambivalence in the work
— it is as if Brecht were trying to win and lose at the same time, to sacrifice
neither his compulsion to present only that which is nor his belief in the
possibility of a future which is no longer a "finstere Zeit." In "Die zwei
Hergaben" this paradox takes its most extreme form: the "Einverständnis" with
death and forgetting, with hopelessness, becomes the necessary condition of
hope. The failure of the individual is subsumed in the progression of history
towards a distant and perhaps unattainable Utopia, and the optimism which
Brecht himself is unable to present in his work may be provided by those he
appeals to so earnestly in "An die Nachgeborenen":

> Ihr, die ihr auftauchen werdet aus der Flut
> In der wir untergegangen sind
> Gedenkt
> Wenn ihr von unsern Schwächen sprecht
> Auch der finsteren Zeit
> Der ihr entronnen seid.[89]

89 GW 9, p. 722

The anti-idealism of his work, of his whole artistic method, must call in question the possibility of a change which is not "natürlich." His need alone cannot provide the justification. Perhaps Herr Keuner is not so different from the man who needs a "god"; his difficulty is the same, that his faith in the external principle, the Archimedean point which he has chosen to move the universe about, is shaken by the knowledge that it is his own hypothesis which puts it there. Herr Keuner is, after all, Herr Brecht.

VI

Der Rückgang ins Animalische bewahrt nicht vor dem Zerrissenwerden und der Rückgang ins Vegetative nicht vor dem Entwurzeltwerden. Der Rückgang ins Anorganische soll vor beiden bewahren ... Doch der Verzicht auf Ziele bietet selbst kein Ziel. Er ist vielleicht eine Möglichkeit zu überwintern, doch nicht zu leben. – Die Bewegungen, die wir beschrieben haben: Flucht vor der Drohung des Identitätsverlustes in Identitätslosigkeit und Flucht vor der Drohung des Nichtsprechenkönnens in Sprachlosigkeit, haben die gleiche Struktur. Beide flüchten sie in das, wovor sie fliehen. Das Ziel der Bewegung, in beiden Fällen, ist Selbstzerstörung. Aber kann Selbstzerstörung ein Ziel sein? [90]

Klaus Heinrich,
Versuch über die Schwierigkeit nein zu sagen

In his attempt to escape from the infinite spiral of his early work, from the narrowing gyres of the "Selbstvernichtungsprozeß," Brecht is faced with a problem of some magnitude in his attitude to his own earlier artistic personality, in that he is unable to reject many of the axioms around which it is constructed. Above all, he refuses to give up the demand for "totality of experience," for a re-creation in art of the "whole world" in which he lives (and indeed, the alternative, a retreat into "Enge und Existentialismus," is rightly characterised

90   Heinrich, op.cit., p. 44

by Peter Szondi as a "Rettungsversuch," not a "Lösungsversuch"[91]) which seems
central to his early work and which Helge Hultberg has analysed in considerable
detail in his important study *Die ästhetischen Anschauungen Bertolt Brechts*.[92]
This "totality" is at the basis of the "naive" aesthetic of the early period; the
unity of the early work is a representational unity gained by reducing a
"totality" of world, whose "one-ness" is taken for granted, through a "naive"
vision into the work of art. "Theater" and "Wirklichkeit," "Kunst" und
"Leben" are really equivalent, art is merely "potenziert," concentrated into
significance, it has no unity of its own, but a derived unity which is the unity of
its "vision" or perspective. The perspective of *Mahagonny* is not "autonomous,"
it is rather "automatic"; the "Verfremdung" which takes place is not so much a
conscious procedure as the result of this "natural" vision reducing reality to the
confines of the individual work. The city of Mahagonny does not "stand for"
the world, in the sense of the later plays; it "is" the world, and this largely
because the author himself has little distance from the world of his play, because
he himself is too clearly involved in it. With the disappearance of the
"autobiographical hero" from the later plays (even if this disappearance is often
more apparent than real) there is an increased distance, a doubling of
perspective. In *Mahagonny* this "perspective" is presented to us without
comment, but in a later work like *Der gute Mensch von Sezuan* the perspective
itself becomes "verfremdet" by the perspective of the author-commentator, who
allies himself with the audience rather than with the play itself. Indeed, in the
later plays it seems often as if the early Brecht has survived on this level of "the
play itself," but is confronted with a wiser, maturer Brecht as commentator,
who tells the audience what this apparently naive procedure *really* means from
his new point of view, and that it is not so much the "representation of reality"
which has changed, but the "interpretation of reality" which is added to it.
Brecht's early artistic practice springs from a natural vision which defies the
translation of "theory" into "reality," and we may perhaps be forgiven for
regarding even Marxism, with its expressed materialism, as nevertheless "theory"
— and in the later plays, it seems often that the "theory" is superimposed on the
works rather than forming an integral part of their structure. As "commentary,"
it "corrects" the direction of the play, in much the same way that Brecht
"corrected" the plays of other writers and his own early work; it does not
disturb the premises (though frequently adding to them), but often arrives at a
radically different conclusion, which, however, seems often to lie "outside" the
work proper, which does not "decide" in its own terms — the audience are
directed towards a decision in the terms of their guide, the "author-commentator," which they may or may not accept without rejecting the "realism" of the

91   Peter Szondi, *Theorie des modernen Dramas,* Frankfurt 1959, pp. 81ff.
92   Copenhagen 1962; cf. esp. pp. 52—98

first level. It is as if we were being presented with the work and at the same time a "Gebrauchsanweisung" in the sense of the *Hauspostille,* a set of rules for applying it to our own condition. In a sense, the degree of ironic "Abstand" already present in this introduction to the *Hauspostille* pre-figures the "double perspective" of the later work; it is an invitation to read the work "gewisser-maßen gegen den Strom"[93] which is at the same time flippant and serious. For Brecht in 1926, the inherent "dangers" of the *Hauspostille* were real enough.

Nor is this self-commentary by any means an isolated phenomenon. Its place in the novels of Thomas Mann and Robert Musil, to name only the two most obvious examples, is too familiar to require comment here. When Musil writes of *Der Mann ohne Eigenschaften* that "die Geschichte dieses Romans kommt darauf hinaus, daß die Geschichte, die in ihm erzählt werden sollte, nicht erzählt wird,"[94] then he is expressing a state of affairs which is not entirely dissimilar to the one in which Brecht finds himself in his later work. It seems curious that Brecht should commit himself to an "epic" theatre at a time when novelists themselves are denying the very possibility of "Erzählen," where the novel is rapidly reaching the stage where it rejects plot as an old-fashioned irrelevance and itself strives to become a kind of "Welttheater," but the contradiction is only a superficial one: Brecht's "commentary," like Mann's and Musil's, springs from a dissatisfaction with the simple form, an insight into its questionability, which forces him to supplement it with a new, relativising viewpoint. Brecht's "epic," like Broch's, returns rather to an earlier tradition, that of the "omniscient" narrator who uses his "story" as the basis for an instruction about the "nature of things" (it is no coincidence that Lucretius became a favourite with the later Brecht). It is the ability of the "Erzähler" to make the otherwise unclear direction of the material world explicit that so appeals to Brecht, his ability to "form" the world to an overall image of the human condition such as we have already discussed. Indeed, in these terms, the "natural vision" of the early Brecht seems something of an anachronism, which in a matter of time must be replaced by a more complex vision. It is as if Brecht had begun at the point where Malte Laurids Brigge would wish to finish, as if he has never had to fight back through the traditional literary consciousness that so inhibits Malte and the earlier Rilke. Perhaps this is genuinely, in Hans Mayer's words, a survival of the "plebeian tradition" in Brecht, a standing outside the normal literary scene which may have owed something to the provinciality of Augsburg and the unusual independence it seems to have produced in Brecht,[95] but it is clear that it could not last for even in the world of Berlin and Munich, nor, as we shall see, is the distance between Brecht and Malte as great as it would at first appear.

---

93 Rilke on *Malte Laurids Brigge, Ausgewählte Briefe I,* p. 363
94 Robert Musil, *Der Mann ohne Eigenschaften,* Hamburg 1958, p. 1640
95 cf. Hans Mayer, *Bertolt Brecht und die Tradition,* Pfullingen 1961, pp. 20ff.

Arnolt Bronnen's already quoted description of the early Brecht as a "Kleinstädter, der mit dem Problem der Großstadt nie ganz fertig wurde" is revealing if we consider it in the light of their respective literary styles: in Bronnen, the "new language" is forced, over-conscious, in Brecht, it seems to be the natural "dialect" of the author. For Bronnen, "opposition" to what has gone before, avoidance of the "artistic" language of the nineteenth century, becomes the main principle of his work; for Brecht, this opposition is a natural result of his own practice, which seems from the first to be "given," to have grown naturally out of his peculiar literary environment. Yet it is only a matter of time before this "natural vision" of the early Brecht destroys itself from within; its premises are too much at variance with the reality of the "große Städte" into which he was projected in the twenties, a reality which overwhelms and annihilates the passivity of its "registrator," whether he be Brecht or Brigge. The claim to present "reality" which is so characteristic of the early aesthetics requires some revision, since "reality" can now only be withstood and comprehended if it is seen as the expression of a given direction, which is, in the last analysis, "projected" into it by the author himself.

In this respect it is instructive to compare Brecht with another "natural writer," and one who exerted considerable influence on the younger Brecht — Georg Büchner. Büchner's rebellion against the art and the aesthetics of his time seems to be based on such similar premises to Brecht's own that it is scarcely surprising that the young Brecht counted Büchner among his favourite authors and that many of his early works show traces of this influence.[96]

Büchner justifies his "artistic revolution" by appealing to "reality" in much the same way that Brecht, in his early theoretical writings, demands a new "sociological relevance" for the drama. In the prose work *Lenz*, Lenz is given the following speech, in which he violently attacks "idealist" theories of art:

> Er sagte: Die Dichter, von denen man sage, sie geben die Wirklichkeit, hätten auch keine Ahnung davon, doch seien sie immer noch erträglicher als die, welche die Wirklichkeit verklären wollten. Er sagte: Der liebe Gott hat die Welt wohl gemacht, wie sie sein soll, und wir können wohl nicht was Besseres klecksen; unser einziges Bestreben soll sein, ihm ein wenig nachzuschaffen. Ich verlange in Allem — Leben, Möglichkeit des Daseins, und dann ist's gut; wir haben nicht zu fragen, ob es schön, ob es häßlich ist. Das Gefühl, daß was geschaffen sei, Leben habe, stehe über diesen beiden und sei das einzige Kriterium in Kunstsachen. Übrigens begegne es uns nur selten, in Shakespeare finden wir es, und in den Volksliedern tönt es einem ganz, in Goethe manchmal entgegen; alles Übrige kann man ins Feuer werfen ...[97]

---

96   cf. Esslin, op.cit., pp. 159—60
97   Georg Büchner, *Werke und Briefe*, Wiesbaden 1958, p. 94

Here Lenz is merely Büchner's mouthpiece — the "idealistische Periode" to which he reacts is, strictly speaking, an anachronism.[98] Yet the full significance of the passage only becomes plain when we consider it in the context of the work; Lenz finds himself in a state of religious crisis, he is possessed by a continual struggle between a despairing atheism and a naive, childlike Christianity, between a totally "meaningful" and a totally "meaningless" existence,[99] and it is in the last resort his inability to reconcile these two extremes (rather than his unhappy love for Friederike) which drives him mad. For Lenz, the creation is either the expression of a universal, divine law, or it is meaningless and absurd. There is, then, a strange irony in the argument with which Lenz justifies his conception of the rôle of art as a kind of "imitatio dei"; the phrase "der liebe Gott hat die Welt wohl gemacht, wie sie sein soll" sounds very odd indeed coming from the author of *Dantons Tod* and *Woyzeck*. Lenz himself meets an end which is scarcely "wie es sein soll." Yet there is no mistaking Büchner's involvement in Lenz's views on "aesthetics." This "imitatio dei" which is for Büchner the basis of all art and is yet itself threatened by "der Fels des Atheismus" is only an expression of one of the most important problems of his work: the reconcilement of human suffering with the idea of a meaningful universe presided over by a just divinity. So Danton despairs before the "gräßlicher Fatalismus der Geschichte,"[100] so Payne disproves the existence of God:

> Schafft das Unvollkommene weg, dann allein könnt ihr Gott demonstrieren; Spinoza hat es versucht. Man kann das Böse leugnen, aber nicht den Schmerz; nur der Verstand kann Gott beweisen, das Gefühl empört sich dagegen. Merke dir es, Anaxagoras: warum leide ich? Das ist der Fels des Atheismus. Das leiseste Zucken des Schmerzes, und rege es sich nur in einem Atom, macht einen Riß in der Schöpfung von oben bis unten.[101]

Yet although Büchner seems more conscious than any of his contemporaries of the "imperfectness" of the world and finds his belief in a meaningful existence imperilled by this consciousness, it is precisely this "unsatisfactory" world which he demands should be presented in art, "ob es schön, ob es häßlich ist." He destroys all traditional aesthetic criteria in favour of a fidelity to 'life' while at the same time presenting "life" in his work as a virtual disproof of the meaningfulness of the universe, a premise on which his argument seems to be based. "Realism" becomes almost a "moral" compulsion for Büchner; he attacks

---

[98] cf. Hans Mayer, *Studien,* Berlin 1955, pp. 143ff.
[99] cf. Wolfgang Martens, "Ideologie und Verzweiflung. Religiöse Motive in Büchners Revolutionsdrama," *Euphorion* 54 (1960), pp. 83—108, which establishes a similar polarity in *Dantons Tod.*
[100] Brief an die Braut, Gießen [November 1833?], p. 374
[101] *Werke und Briefe,* p. 53

"idealism" as "die schändlichste Verachtung der menschlichen Natur." The writer has a moral obligation to present the world "as it is" — yet we have already seen that the source of his obligation is deeply ambiguous. Lenz sees it as an "imitatio dei," but it would seem that Büchner, like Lenz, remains caught between the poles of his own argument.

In the "Probevorlesung," *Über Schädelnerven*, which Büchner wrote for Zürich University in the last year of his short life, the implications of this morally-charged "realism" become clearer. In the methodological introduction to the lecture he distinguishes between two scientific "methods," the "teleological" and the "philosophical." Of the former he writes:

> Die größtmöglichste Zweckmäßigkeit ist das einzige Gesetz der teleologischen Methode; nun fragt man aber natürlich nach dem Zwecke dieses Zweckes, und so macht sie auch ebenso natürlich bei jeder Frage einen Progressus in infinitum . . . [102]

This "Zweckmäßigkeit" Büchner rejects in much the same way that Marx was later to reject the "idealism" of Hegel's dialectic — with the claim that it is "upside-down." For the method which Büchner advocates, the "philosophical" method, the situation is reversed:

> Die Natur handelt nicht nach Zwecken, sie reibt sich nicht in einer unendlichen Reihe von Zwecken auf, von denen der eine den anderen bedingt; sondern sie ist in allen ihren Äußerungen sich unmittelbar selbst genug. Alles, was da ist, ist um seiner selbst willen da. Das Gesetz dieses Seins zu suchen, ist das Ziel der der teleologischen gegenüberstehenden Ansicht, die ich die *philosophische* nennen will. Alles, was für *jene* Zweck ist, wird für *diese* Wirkung. Wo die teleologische Schule mit ihrer Antwort fertig ist, fängt die Frage für die philosophische an. Diese Frage, die uns auf allen Punkten anredet, kann ihre Antwort nur in einem Grundgesetz für die gesamte Organisation finden, und so wird für die philosophische Methode das ganze körperliche Dasein des Individuums nicht zu seiner eigenen Erhaltung aufgebracht, sondern es wird die Manifestation eines Urgesetzes, eines Gesetzes der Schönheit, das nach den einfachsten Rissen und Linien die höchsten und reinsten Formen hervorbringt. Alles, Form und Stoff, ist für sie an dies Gesetz gebunden. [103]

The "imitatio dei" of *Lenz* is here expanded into a belief in an "Urgesetz der Schönheit," which governs the whole of matter and therefore automatically supersedes distinctions between "schön" and "häßlich," since the socalled "häßlich" is itself a product of the law, and we merely lack an adequate

---

102 op.cit., p. 350
103 loc.cit.

technique to observe the application of the law to it. We are immediately reminded of the passage in *Lenz* where Büchner seems to foreshadow his method in *Woyzeck:*

> Man versuche es einmal und senke sich in das Leben des Geringsten und gebe es wieder in den Zuckungen, den Andeutungen, dem ganzen feinen, kaum bemerkten Mienenspiel ... Man muß die Menschheit lieben, um in das eigentümliche Wesen jedes einzudringen; es darf keiner zu gering, keiner zu häßlich sein, erst dann kann man sie verstehen; das unbedeutendste Gesicht macht einen tiefern Eindruck als die bloße Empfindung des Schönen ...[104]

In his literary work too Büchner is in pursuit of an "Urgesetz des Schönen," but the "sign" of this universal law seems to waver under the influence of the pessimism which results from his attempt to approach this "totality of experience" through the simple and oppressed. As in *Dantons Tod,* the problem of suffering disturbs the balance of a system based on an "Urgesetz der Schönheit," it "splits the creation from top to bottom," and the "law" refuses to reveal itself. In *Woyzeck,* most particularly, the "positive" "Grundgesetz" of Büchner's lecture seems to be replaced by a negativity which finds its most extreme and archetypal expression in the Grandmother's parable. Between this affirmative theory, with its justification of all life as the product of a sublime law, and the world of Büchner's victim-heroes there is a remarkable conflict.

Büchner's "Grundgesetz" destroys itself; the "Leben" which he represents does not support his own theory, which comes after all to bear the same relation to his work as the works of the "idealists" to reality. The compulsion to present reality "as it is" leads to an insight which destroys the justification of this compulsion. It would seem that the "law" must either be inverted or abandoned, if it is to be brought into agreement with the realities of his literary production. In fact, Büchner's works seem to be governed by a "negative dialectic" not unlike that of the young Brecht — there is the same Rousseau-like dream of an original unity with nature which has been lost, the same progression towards a tragic stasis through the manifestation of an evil principle of existence, a perpetual decadence. Indeed, Danton sees life only as a more complex, chaotic form of decay than death, in words which are not unreminiscent of the "Sonett über schlechtes Leben:"

> Ja, wer an Vernichtung glauben könnte! dem wäre geholfen. — Da ist keine Hoffnung im Tod: er ist nur eine einfachere, das Leben eine verwickeltere, organisierte Fäulnis, das ist der ganze Unterschied![105]

For Büchner, too, "das Chaos ist aufgebraucht." His revolution, which attempts to "restore" the good, produces only more evil, "frißt ihre eignen Kinder." For

104   op.cit., pp. 94—5
105   op.cit., p. 67

Danton, a historical optimism of the kind that lies behind Marx's dialectic is impossible. It is the loss of this optimism which Büchner's work comes increasingly to represent.

It is instructive to consider the parallelism of Büchner's views with those of the younger Brecht: the demand for a "new realism" joined paradoxically to a world view whose extreme pessimism seems to undermine the very basis of this compulsion to show the world "as it is." It is, we have seen, possible to reduce the early work of Brecht to a similar "natural idealism" gone wrong, to a belief in a "Grundgesetz" which "devours its own children" like Büchner's revolution. Brecht shares, too, with Büchner his demand for "totality of experience" in the work of art, for an art which is able to reproduce the entire consciousness of a society which can no longer find itself in the "classics," and his rejection of these works as "unreal." In this respect it is interesting to compare Brecht's argument in an open letter to the sociologist Fritz Sternberg, published in June 1927 under the provocative title *Sollten wir nicht die Ästhetik liquidieren?* :

> Der ästhetische Standpunkt wird der neuen Produktion, auch wenn er lobende Äußerungen ergibt, nicht gerecht. Dies wird bewiesen durch einen kurzen Blick auf nahezu sämtliche Aktionen zugunsten der neuen Dramatik. Auch wo der Instinkt die Kritik richtig leitete, konnte sie aus dem ästhetischen Vokabularium nur wenig überzeugende Belege für ihre positive Einstellung erbringen ... Die neue Produktion, die mehr und mehr das große epische Theater heraufführt, das der soziologischen Situation entspricht, kann zunächst ihrem Inhalt wie ihrer Form nach nur von denjenigen verstanden werden, die diese Situation verstehen. Sie wird die alte Ästhetik nicht befriedigen, sondern sie wird sie vernichten.[106]

Brecht rejects the "aesthetic standpoint" in much the same way that Büchner in *Lenz* rejects the categories "schön" and "häßlich," as bound up with a concept of art which no longer corresponds to the "reality" which he wishes to convey in his works. For Brecht, the present-day drama has "keinen soziologischen Raum mehr," and the "old" aesthetics which were deduced from its practice can no longer be of relevance for the "new production." While the hope seems to be implied that eventually these outdated views may be replaced by a new and radically opposed system which is capable of understanding the "new" drama in its relation to the "new" reality, Brecht stresses that at present "der Soziologe ist unser Mann," that we must "do without" aesthetics, and judge the work rather as if it were a scientific description of modern society. The new drama may well have a "new" form, but this cannot be described in terms of the old criteria, which are seen as being conditioned by the demands of a different society, the society of the 300 years since Shakespeare, "in denen das

106 GW 15, p. 1268

Individuum sich zum Kapitalisten entwickelte." Brecht sees the Shakespearean drama as the basis on which the old aesthetics of drama have been constructed, but claims that they are now outmoded, "überwunden nicht durch das, was auf den Kapitalismus folgt, sondern durch den Kapitalismus selber." The development of the society which the Shakespearean drama heralded has made them meaningless — the "great individual" has been eliminated by the world of late capitalism. So not only is a radically new type of drama required, which will stand in the same relation to our world as Shakespeare's plays to theirs, but this drama must itself produce its aesthetic justification, which must, as it were, grow out of the new dramatic practice.

For all Brecht's "historicism," his attack on traditional aesthetics clearly springs from similar motives to Büchner's. Büchner's criticism of the "idealist" is in effect the same as Brecht's criticism of the present-day drama, that it fails to represent the present-day world, that its concept of "reality" does not correspond to the "totality" of modern consciousness that both claim to speak for. Büchner too wishes to produce a literature which has "soziologischen Raum." Brecht's anticipation of a "new aesthetic" does not conceal the fact that for him "aesthetics" is a secondary problem, a problem of description rather than prescription, a state of affairs which does not change substantially even in the later theoretical writings. We have already seen that his early artistic practice seems to correspond rather to Büchner's dictum of a creation in the work of art of "Leben, Möglichkeit des Daseins," to the translation of a unified "vision" of reality into the individual work. Brecht's justification of this principle of "realism" seems at this stage as ambiguous as Büchner's — both reject "idealism," that is, any system which starts from the "ideal" in its attempt to interpret the "real," yet at the same time their "realism" seems itself, despite its "materialistic" surface, to spring from an "idealistic" point of origin: a concept of a lost unity, "eins sein mit Allem," which demands to be restored consciously and by definition cannot be. And so their "artistic method," their "realism," is forced to prove increasingly the impossibility of their "ideal" state, the impossibility of ever re-creating the "Utopia" which lies behind them, and demonstrates rather the inevitable movement with which the world about them distances itself from this "ideal." It is hard to visualise the type of work which Büchner might have produced after *Woyzeck*, just as it is hard to see, for Brecht, any possible further development of the world of *Mahagonny*. The full destructiveness of the "Grundgesetz" has been realised, and it must be replaced by some new construction which allows the writer to "move" once more. Büchner's death-bed insight into the "problem of pain" which so dominates his work might have served as a new starting-point of this kind.[107]

Both Brecht and Büchner are subject to what we might term the "imperative of matter"; the new insight into "reality" which they claim for themselves is

107 cf. *Werke und Briefe*, p. 580

based firmly on a materialistic conception of the world and of history, and it is this "passionate materialism" which remains the single most important characteristic of Brecht's work both before and after his "conversion" to Marxism. Yet the form in which this imperative is applied to the work of art is different for the two writers: in Brecht, the work of art comes close to being allowed importance only as an interpretation of its "society"; in Büchner, it is able to achieve a quality of "Leben" which is in the last resort autonomous and timeless. Büchner's rejection of any "social limitation" in art is not merely "historical," as Brecht's at first glance appears to be, it is a much wider appeal, for a "natural," "naive" art which presents the world "as it is" as against a "sentimental," "philosophical" art which applies intellectual categories to life rather than deriving them from it.

The peculiar difficulty of Brecht's position in the late twenties seems to stem from the fact that he too, like Büchner, is a "natural" writer, but that having reached an ultimate contradiction comparable to that inherent in Büchner's last works, he is forced to rationalise his procedure and his aims in order to escape the implications of his own system. Thus it often seems that the actual process of "writing" remains to the last for Brecht something simply "selbstverständlich," that it springs from an unchanging "compulsion" to present the world "as it is," and that the optimism of Marx comes to stand in a similar relation to the later works to that between Büchner's "Grundgesetz" and his own artistic practice. The "meaningfulness" of the world may be assumed by these theories, but in the plays, it must each time be proved by the weighing of a mass of conflicting evidence; for Brecht, the conclusions on which the theories are based are worthless if they are not, like Büchner's "Gesetz," to be deduced from the realities of an existence which Brecht, like Büchner, seeks above all to examine from the point of view of the "geringe Leute," the victims of society who demonstrate its character more surely than the outmoded "heroes" of a Shakespearean drama. This is not to deny the importance of Brecht's theories, but merely to stress their "paradigmatic" quality; their ideal "meaningfulness," their "certainty of direction" stands in much the same relation to Brecht's artistic practice as Marx's "classless society" to the present realities of socialism. In the plays this paradigm is overridden by the compulsion to present a "concrete" truth, and not an ideal one; "reality" does not keep pace with the "law" which the writer would gladly deduce from it, and the pessimism which led us in the first place to the new "optimism" remains an equal partner in the argument, which must first be satisfied if the "optimism" is to retain its validity. Much of the "evidence" remains unchanged; indeed, we shall see that "ambivalent evidence" of this kind is typical of the later work and that the conclusions Brecht asks us to draw from his later plays seem often imperilled by the weight of the arguments he himself has amassed against them, the arguments, as often as not, of the young Brecht.

In this search by a "natural writer" for a new perspective which can liberate him from the stasis he has reached while allowing him to preserve the basic character of his art, the attractions of Marxism are obvious. The naive "Grundgesetz" of the early period can be replaced by a positive and conscious system which succeeds in combining a not un-Brechtian materialism with an optimistic progression whose idealism is at least well-disguised. Without surrendering this materialism and the "realist compulsion" that lies behind it, Brecht is able to take over a philosophy which draws radically different conclusions from similar premises, which turns his "negative dialectic" upside-down even more neatly than it had done Hegel's. Consciousness becomes, instead of a principle of decay and destruction, a positive, optimistic force, destined to transform the world gradually in the direction of a distant, perhaps even ultimately unattainable communistic Utopia, in a direction which remains positive even if the world has to "get worse to get better," even if the individual is never able to see this "progress" within his own life-span. In the end, the "good" will triumph.

In his "materialisation" of Hegel, Marx transforms the "positive" direction of Hegel's dialectic from a postulate of the idealist consciousness to a "law of nature," a so-called "scientific truth" (whatever that may mean). This claim for "scientific truth" (which explains to a very large extent the attraction of Marx's system for Brecht) is, however, precisely that aspect of Marx's theory which has been most subject to attack and to "revision." Hegel's construction, which is idealistic, has no need to prove its assumption of an original "good" thesis which gradually realises itself more and more; for him, the "consciousness" is itself "real," and to have analysed the direction of consciousness and the "method" by which it works, to have given this "consciousness" a "good" direction, is by definition to have given the world a "good" direction, as it is the consciousness which expresses and directs the world, to the extent that "Geist," in the form of the "Weltgeist," becomes virtually a divine principle. We may be unprepared to accept the direction of Hegel's dialectic, but we could never say it was "wrong"; to accept the "good" direction of Hegel's dialectic is to accept its idealistic basis, that it is the consciousness and not a function of "matter" itself which determines the world. Marx, however, seems to put himself in a less easily defensible position by his "taking-over" of this positive progression almost without question, as the "natural law" of civilisation. As a materialist, he derives the "laws of consciousness" from material factors, the consciousness itself becomes material and subject to the same laws as "matter." To claim, then, that this positive progression is inherent in nature and in man's nature, is, however, to expose oneself to criticism from materialists as an idealist; Marx's positive view of history can be opposed by an equally materialist analysis with a "negative" direction, or indeed, by one which fails to see any direction at all; in this respect his debt to Hegel's idealism becomes plain. For Marx, the triumph of the proletariat is not only inevitable but also "good," but it is possible to accept its inevitability without its "goodness," to postulate its "goodness" and deny its invevitability, or to deny both. In this respect his system, which claims to "materialise" Hegel, seems to have failed, in that it is as dependent as Hegel's on a direction which is "implanted" by consciousness, which is not inherent in the phenomena themselves. Beside this problem, the question of truth or untruth of Marx's "Gesellschaftswissenschaft" seems merely secondary; the "direction" which we give to history remains speculation, it remains, as with Hegel, an act of consciousness, not a "law of nature" capable of demonstration. It is, however, wrong to assume, like Hultberg,[108] that because at this point an element of "free will" is introduced into the system, the system itself is destroyed; it merely reveals itself as not a law but a hypothesis — a hypothesis which can by no means be taken lightly, since its flexibility and its dialectic structure allow for a "reversal of proof" at any stage. The individual who rejects this hypothesis has not, as Hultberg seems to be claiming, "disproved" it — it is equally possible that the hypothesis will "disprove" him, that he will find himself on the historically "wrong" side. Marx's logic goes beyond the formal world of the Aristotelians — it is, fundamentally, an idealistic logic like Hegel's.

Nevertheless, the fact that Marxism demands such an exercise of positive consciousness remains its chief difficulty for Brecht, as his need for it arises from a crisis in which the individual consciousness seems to run the risk of being eliminated completely. In this dialectic of "Selbstvernichtung" and "Selbst-erhaltung," however, the individual consciousness has a vital role to play. If its "negativity" is to be absorbed into the new "positive consciousness," the "communal consciousness" of Marxism, it must first "identify itself" as that which is to be re-integrated, and show that the decision is a logical growth of the self which has existed to date. Brecht, however, seems determined at first to attempt another strategy; to destroy the early "Ich" altogether and to begin again.

We have seen how Brecht is concerned in his early work with attaining an "equivalence" between art and reality, with "removing" the art-character of the work in order to stress its direct relation to life, its "Möglichkeit des Daseins," and how, at the same time, this reality grows too strong for its "registrator," how the destructive spiral which he sees in the world about him takes possession of his own existence and reduces him to the "end-stasis" of *Mahagonny* and the *Sonette,* where the individual is "condemned" and executed by a hostile society and a hostile nature acting together. The "realist compulsion" which we have analysed becomes a trap from which the author cannot escape: he is the victim of his own insight into the meaningless absurdity of the world which he has bound himself to represent in his work. In the last resort he is faced with the

---

108   Hultberg, op.cit., pp. 139ff.

reality of an anarchical universe against which the individual is unable to assert himself. His artistic "code" forbids him to react consciously against this meaninglessness; the "meaning" must be found in the universe itself, and not merely projected onto it by the author. The rejection of "consciousness" which we have seen to be one of the important characteristics of Brecht's early work, leads in the final works of the early period to a thorough-going "destruction" of the individual consciousness, an end-stasis which makes individuality meaningless. For all the differences in the quality of their "realism," there is a remarkable parallel between this "loss of identity" in Brecht and the difficulties of Malte Laurids Brigge/Rilke in his attempt to "see" the world about him, to "discover" the things around him by freeing himself from the prejudices of "consciousness." For Malte, as for the young Brecht, this desire to see the world "as it is" results in a rejection of the self, a rejection of the individual consciousness, which leads him into a "Selbstvernichtungsprozeß" not dissimilar to that of the Sonette. Malte becomes "ein Nichts," but this "Nichts" threatens his existence in any shape or form; the novel is dominated by a kind of spiritual "horror vacui." In a perceptive essay on Malte, Ulrich Fülleborn analyses the position which Rilke has reached in this work in terms which make its relevance to Brecht and to the problems of modern literature in general clear:

> ... der fehlende Aufbau im Sinne der Architektur des klassischen Romans verweist auf den Ausfall des Erzählers, der noch aus selbstbewußter Subjektivität Ordnung zu stiften vermochte. Jetzt erzählt nicht mehr ein Ich, sondern die Wirklichkeit diktiert. Sie hat es auf die Destruktion des "Helden" angelegt, die Entthronung des Menschen als Subjekt, seine völlige Degradierung, sofern er sich als autonome Persönlichkeit behaupten will.[109]

This opposition of "Wirklichkeit" and "Persönlichkeit" is, as we have seen, thoroughly characteristic of the young Brecht, and the destruction of the "autonomous personality" which Fülleborn sees in Malte is carried out with even greater thoroughness in the works we have analysed. Brecht shares with Rilke/Malte the desire for "eine neue Totalität, nicht eine vom Ich aus nach überkommenen Allgemeinbegriffen konstruierte 'falsche Utopie,' sondern eine aperspektivische Welt, mit offenen Horizonten," yet the "Perspektive des Nichts, das denkt"[110] which becomes Malte's solution to the problem remains for him an impossibility, a contradiction, as to "think" is to identify himself absolutely (cogito ergo sum!), and he is threatened even more by his own self-destructive tendencies than by "die Wirklichkeit." For Brecht as for Rilke, the revolt against a "false Utopia" of outmoded generalisations in art and society demands the

109   Ulrich Fülleborn, "Form und Sinn der 'Aufzeichnungen des Malte Laurids Brigge'," Unterscheidung und Bewahrung, Festschrift für Hermann Kunisch, Berlin 1961, p. 161.
110   op.cit., p. 167

"Destruierung der alten Formgesetze" in order to clear the way for a "Rekomposition," and the "Perspektive des Nichts" figures as prominently in this process for the Brecht of *Mahagonny* as for Malte.

We have already seen the dangers of this "Perspektive des Nichts" for Brecht. The loss of a personal consciousness is the last step in the "Selbstvernichtungs-prozeß," the artist destroys his consciousness in the attempt to evade the constant barrage to which it is subjected. He becomes able to "think" like nature itself, the world "thinks" through his nothingness, and his self is reduced to the function of a camera, a reproducing medium. At the same time, by surrendering itself, it progresses inevitably towards the "Nichts," which it has chosen as "perspective," this "neutral" consciousness becomes a negative consciousness, and finally a loss of consciousness, a retreat into namelessness and speech-lessness. The crisis which followed *Malte* assumes with Brecht an even more extreme form; paradoxically, "speechlessness" itself becomes literature. The "Lehrstücke" employ a language which has become depersonalised, where every word has to be justified against the imperative of speechlessness which seems to lie behind these works. We have seen how the "Am besten du bleibst sitzen / Und wartest auf das Ende" of *Mahagonny* is a demonstration of the pointlessness of literature as well as the hopelessness of society; indeed, it is in *Mahagonny* that the crisis of speechlessness begins to make itself felt, together with the rejection of the individual consciousness.

The "loss of identity" which is such a striking characteristic of Brecht's first Marxist works seems in many ways a further development of this "rejection of consciousness." "Meaning" is suddenly given to the hitherto meaningless universe, but the individual who is responsible for this "revaluation" attempts to conceal himself. There is a tendency throughout these works to disregard the individual consciousness as a factor in the situation, or even to treat it as a positively harmful quantity which must, as in *Die Maßnahme*, be eliminated. Brecht tends to destroy the "wrong consciousness" of the early work rather than to correct it. Yet at the same time it is clear that the desire to "disappear" which informs these works, the desire to become anonymous and "unkenntlich" is closely related to the "Selbstvernichtungsprozeß" of the early work; it is an attempt to survive by avoiding the self-exposure which we have seen to be so typical of Jimmy/Paul and the other early Brecht heroes, to escape from the "spiral" by shedding the "personality" like a snake-skin, by having no "Gesicht," no identifiable characteristics for the "storm" to act on. On the surface, it is a retreat from the stoic nihilism of *Mahagonny* and "Vom armen B. B.," a determination to weather the hurricane and not to perish with it, yet this "strategy of survival" seems, more often than not, not so much to "rescue" the threatened self of the early work as to complete its destruction, to eliminate the self completely.

VII

In this period of crisis, *Die heilige Johanna der Schlachthöfe* occupies a remarkable position; although overtly concerned with many of the same problems as the early "Lehrstücke," it has certain peculiar characteristics which cause us to look both forward and backward: a "stoffliche Fülle" and an élan which remind us very much of the earlier plays, joined with a dramatic shape and a utilisation of certain devices which strongly anticipate Brecht's practice in his last and most famous plays. It retains something of a privileged position among his output; although its beginnings reach back to 1926, it remained to the end one of Brecht's favourites, and indeed, it often seems as if in *Johanna* he had achieved at first attempt a solution to the problem of writing the particular type of Marxist play he wished to write which refused to repeat itself for a number of years, despite all efforts to the contrary. *Johanna* is somehow immune from the embargo on personality which has been applied so strictly in *Die Maßnahme* and *Der Jasager;* it is altogether curious how, in the initial stages of Brecht's positive phase, he seems able to create only female characters of any vitality — it is only later that the Galileis and the Azdaks appear. Perhaps it is not unreasonable to assume that for Brecht a male characterisation meant, as ever, primarily a self-portrait, and that at this stage he was unprepared to expose himself in this way, whereas the female roles show a realism and a lack of inhibition of this kind which seems similarly to be related to their "model," Brecht's wife, Helene Weigel. It seems often as if Brecht were purposely distancing himself from his problem in the shape of a female heroine — be that as it may, the influence of this type of female role on the entire later development of his theatre is enormous. We shall see later the extent to which many of Johanna's characteristics appear later once more in Shen Te and Grusche Vachnadze. Even in the last plays, "goodness" is inevitably the prerogative of the "heroine"; Brecht's "heroes" are all far too ambivalent to be good. In the naivety of the simple heroines, Johanna or Pelagea Wlassowa, Shen Te or Grusche, is a quality which is somehow immune to the ordeals of the "Niemandsein," and identifies them clearly, not as "no-ones," but as people. Brecht's heroes all compromise themselves by their excessive skill in strategy; his heroines are destroyed by their lack of guile, yet somehow this destruction seems to carry more hope with it than the often colourless survival of the others.

We can see *Johanna*, then, as providing a kind of opposite example in the midst of Brecht's most difficult phase, as a foretaste of the solutions he was to favour later and, indeed, of the whole structure of the "dialectic theatre." If I have chosen not to include a full analysis of this very important play here, then only because the excellent essay of Käthe Rülicke[111] seems to make such an

---

[111] "Die heilige Johanna der Schlachthöfe," *Sinn und Form* 11 (1959), pp. 429ff.

extensive analysis superfluous — let us restrict ourselves, then, to a discussion of the theme and of the main interpretative problems.

Johanna represents a solution to Brecht's problem of writing a "Marxist" drama which he was to employ again and again: the method of "negative proof." The actual "Wendung zum Marxismus" is not represented, as it had been, albeit in highly symbolic form, in the *Badener Lehrstück;* instead, Brecht does his best to convince us, through an analysis of the society of the present with Marxist insights, of the necessity of such a "Wendung." The "act of consciousness," the "jump" of which we spoke is not represented, we are left ourselves to supply it as the logical outcome of the play. There is no longer any attempt to produce the "good collective" itself on the stage, as at the present stage of the dialectic this "good collective" remains invisible, so to speak in its "Niemandsgestalt," and only the future can give it shape. Meanwhile, the present may give grounds for hope. The insight into the "early phase" of the dialectic ("Das Ziel lag in großer Ferne") seems to prohibit the creation of a falsely Utopian conclusion as strongly as the unwillingness of the young Brecht to present "false Utopias" of this kind as art, his overriding rejection of "illusion." Only in one play does Brecht ever really attempt this kind of "Durchbruch" — in *Die Mutter,* where it is already "given" by his source, the novel of the same name by Maxim Gorky, and even here the triumph of the revolutionary party with which the work concludes is more symbolic than real. The method employed in *Johanna* remains typical of the later dramatic practice.

Johanna herself, as we have seen, is a new type of Brechtian protagonist, even if she shows certain links with the guileless Galy Gay; she is the "guter Mensch" who is ruined by the harsh reality of society, but from whose predicament we, the audience, may deduce the necessity to change it. Indeed, it is the comparison with Shen Te, "der gute Mensch von Sezuan," that immediately springs to mind. Like Shen Te, Johanna is brought by her "goodness," her naive belief in humanity, into an intolerable situation of contradiction and despair which she herself is unable to solve and falls victim to, a kind of sacrifice for the future. Of all Brecht's later heroines, only Grusche in *Der kaukasische Kreidekreis* is rescued from this predicament, rescued by chance masquerading as the "judge" Azdak, who establishes "justice" almost by mistake; yet even here, all the indications point to Grusche's failure and ruin. The "happy ending" is an exception, almost a mistake; for once Brecht presents us with what Ernst Bloch would have called a "Wunschbild des erfüllten Augenblicks," but almost against his own better knowledge. Great stress is laid on the fact that "things don't happen this way." *Der kaukasische Kreidekreis* shows an odd conflict in Brecht, which we shall have cause to treat more fully in Chapter Three: the desire for a "happy ending" for once coupled with a lack of conviction of its possibility, or at least of its possibility in his own life and work, which springs directly from the "pessimism" of the early period. The "solution" of *Kreidekreis* is so riskily balanced and the "special" quality of Grusche's case so carefully demonstrated that it acquires the character of a fairy-tale, a representation not of what is, but what should be. It is as if Brecht has become very tired and allowed the good to win as he wishes it to, but knew it could not, excusing himself for this flight from realism by translating the whole into the world of poetry and the "Märchen."

Johanna finds no such chance solution; from the first she is unequal to the task she has chosen, to "convert" the world by her own good will. Brecht demonstrates with great clarity, and yet with sympathy, the inadequacy of her concepts and the inadequacy of her ability to "learn." Johanna's insight arrives too late, when her "good will" has already been exploited by Mauler and his class in their own best interests. Like the historical St. Joan, her fate is to be used by others; her goodness lacks the discrimination of the good cause, the knowledge which is required to place it at the service of the "good collective." Thus her aims are not realised in the results of her actions; instead of "improving" the world by the "help" which she brings, she merely plays into the hands of the unjust order which rules, by providing an ornament for the ideological "Überbau" which this order uses to conceal the anarchy by which it lives. Mauler is an expert in the fabrication of such false motives — he renders Johanna not merely harmless, but actually useful to the cause which she in fact opposes, the continuing triumph of the capitalists. The dangers of "Hilfe" and the omnipresence of "Gewalt" which had been schematically presented in the *Badener Lehrstück* are here clothed in a "real action" which makes their significance clear. On this level, it becomes apparent that there is a very real political problem involved, a problem with which many German Communists were preoccupied in these years: the building of a united Socialist front against the National Socialists, a union of "gute Menschen" against the Fascist menace. For the social democrats, such an alliance remained to the last suspect, for the same reasons that Johanna gives for her failure to carry out the commission with which she is entrusted:

> Ich will weggehen. Es kann nicht gut sein, was mit Gewalt gemacht wird. Ich gehöre nicht zu ihnen. Hätten mich als Kind der Tritt des Elends und der Hunger Gewalt gelehrt, würde ich zu ihnen gehören und nichts fragen. So aber muß ich weggehen.[112]

The play reads like an attempt to refute these arguments, to demonstrate the necessity of a united front against "Gewalt," even if it is necessary to resort to "Gewalt" oneself. Johanna's problems are "bürgerlich," as Schuhmacher claims,[113] but at this stage these bourgeois problems were a vital concern of the

---

112 GW 2, pp. 753—4
113 Schuhmacher, op.cit., pp. 434ff., *passim*.

Communist Party. In 1932 Ernst Bloch analysed the difficulties of German
Communism in terms of "Ungleichzeitigkeit,"[114] a different rate of growth in
different classes, and saw a new and major political factor in the depression of
the *petite bourgeoisie,* which had in many ways suffered as much as the
proletariat from the economic crisis and had itself become politically active. It is
in this "Kleinbürgertum" that Bloch sees the real strength of Nazism, and he
stresses that, to achieve its political aims, the Communist Party must succeed in
allying itself to the aims and wishes of this class via the social democrats. Marx
and Engels had seen the revolution primarily as a revolution of the proletariat,
but already Lenin had been obliged to ally himself temporarily with the
moderate Socialist Revolutionaries, in order to achieve power, even if only to rid
himself of them later. The extremism of the German Communist Party and its
inability to attain a *modus vivendi* with the socialists was at least partly
responsible for the failure of the "progressive" forces in Germany to halt
Nazism.

In *Johanna,* Brecht seems to be attempting to overcome a corresponding fear
of alliance on Johanna's part, a fear as "guter Mensch" to throw in her lot with
the communists, by a demonstration of the necessity of direct action against the
common enemy. For this reason alone, it is very dangerous to identify Brecht's
"problems" too extensively with the problems of his "heroine," as has often
been done. Brecht may have been bourgeois in origin, but one could scarcely say
that he approached Marxism through Johanna's naive goodness, through the
Salvation Army! Johanna's naivety is not Brecht's, it is the problem which he is
attempting to solve in this play for the sake of others, rather than for himself.
To reject as "bürgerlich" a work which attempts to explain in this way a major
political difficulty of the time, an attempt at "Brückenschlagen," is pure
dogmatism. The argument for Marxism which Brecht presents is perfectly
orthodox. It is the failure of the "moderates," the "good people" to change the
world by wishing alone which he is anxious to demonstrate, and to demonstrate
sympathetically, in order that they may "learn," like the "Monteure" of the
Lehrstück, to throw in their lot with the collective. In 1930 it was surely
preferable to sympathise with the political difficulties of one's own possible
allies and to attempt to show a solution than to dismiss difficulties and allies
alike as "bürgerlich." (Nor does it seem any more logical today, when such
catch-words are even harder to define.)

It seems, then, that one of the major problems we are faced with in reading
Johanna is to avoid a too facile equation of the problems of its heroine and its
author, to realise that her experience is not necessarily his. This is, in fact,
perhaps the first play Brecht has written in which his protagonist is *not* merely a
mouth-piece, a play which shows every sign of the liberating effect of this new

114   *Erbschaft dieser Zeit,* Frankfurt 1962, pp. 104ff.

type of protagonist, and it is inappropriate that he should be charged with the faults which he has projected in this new way. To do so is not simply an expression of political dogmatism — it is a critical error.

The greatest critical difficulty in the play remains, however, the study of the implications of this method of "negative proof," which we have seen to be Brecht's solution to writing a Marxist drama which is at the same time realistic, true to the "realistic compulsion" we have analysed in the earlier Brecht, and yet allows the possibility of an "optimistic" conclusion, if outside the play proper. It is a problem which will continue to occupy us throughout our treatment of the later Brecht and which is ultimately reducible to the dialectic of optimism and pessimism which is described in the final chapter of this work. Johanna, like Anna Fierling later, momentarily attains an insight into the workings of the world which threatens to annihilate her: —

> Ich sehe dies System, und äußerlich
> Ist's lang bekannt, nur nicht im
> Zusammenhang! . . .[115]

but like Courage again, she loses this insight, and it is only in the final scene, when it is useless, that it returns. She has failed; admittedly, unlike Courage, she becomes aware of her failure and of the reason for it — but only when it is too late.

Brecht's thesis is, then, that the audience will learn from Johanna's mistake, that they will learn to act otherwise. But have Johanna's problems been solved? She is presented with a "choice of evils," force against force. To identify with one or the other of them, she will have to be convinced that it leads to "good," or at least to an improvement of the existing conditions, further, that such an improvement is in fact possible. In the crisis situation of the play, the decision is simplified. In accordance with Marx's analysis of a crisis in the capitalist business cycle, which Brecht attempts here to reproduce exactly ("Ich stecke acht Schuh tief im *Kapital*"[116]), the opposites grow so far apart, the antagonism becomes so intense, that revolution or apocalypse seem the only possibilities. *Johanna,* like *Mahagonny,* represents a world in which the dictatorship of force has come out into the open, where the basic anarchy of the system has broken out, and it may well be that this is in fact a reasonable image of the historical situation in Germany at the time of their composition. It remains, however, an exception; in retrospect, Brecht's analysis of the situation and his "open ending" lend themselves quite as easily to a "tragic" interpretation: Johanna's sacrifice has been in vain, the system will in fact continue in one form or another, the open anarchy will retreat into the obscurity from which it came, as it is not in the

115 GW 2, p. 749
116 Hauptmann, op.cit., p. 243

interests of the system itself to provoke such a choice of evils. However "aktuell" *Johanna* may have been at the time, it is precisely the "special quality" of the situation which it presents which limits its argument; Brecht comes, in fact, dangerously close to the effect of the classical tragedy which he satirises so savagely in the verse diction of the play. The open ending of *Johanna* leaves us with precisely the problem which it seeks to solve: "Has Johanna any real alternative? ," because it demands to be "supplemented" by more evidence, it asks to be related to the crisis which it represents. There is a limit to the transference we can make. Perhaps Brecht's "joke" before the Committee on Un-American Activities becomes less of a joke in retrospect:

> I have written a number of plays and poems and songs and plays in the fight against Hitler and, of course, they can be considered, therefore, as revolutionary because I, of course, was for the overthrow of that government.[117]

In many ways, Brecht's support for the official East German doctrine of West German "Revanchismus" in the later years of his life seems similarly to spring from an unwillingness to desert the original basis of his "opposition," the rejection of a "heightened" capitalism in National Socialist Germany. The "choice of evils" becomes greatly simplified if one can "prove" that Adenauer is Hitler and Siemens is really Pierpont Mauler.

Nevertheless, *Johanna,* for all its location in the midst of a personal and political crisis, will remain one of the most successful of Brecht's plays, and again, we wonder if there is not a certain amount of Keunerian cunning behind its success, however patent. The open ending allows an open interpretation; history (and the reader) may give one or other conclusion, the play remains undisturbed, a "forerunner" of the revolution or, to use Ernst Wendt's felicitous phrase, "Trauer über die Unmöglichkeit von Revolution,"[118] a tragedy of society. Though we may cavil at the exaggerations of *Johanna,* Brecht seems here to have solved one of the major problems of the "Tendenzstück" in an exemplary way; it is not imperilled by history, it expresses the desire and not the result, and the result cannot make it irrelevant. At the same time, this openness may tend to inhibit its "political" value — the audience are not told that a solution is possible, they are merely shown that it is desirable. This tends, as we shall see in the next chapter, to give a "timeless" quality to the sufferings of Brecht's heroes and heroines which may militate against hope rather than supporting it. Brecht's unwillingness to present his "optimism" in the work itself tends all too often to "save" his works on a level he himself did not seem to have

---

117   cf. *Brecht. A Collection of Critical Essays,* ed. P. Demetz, Englewood Cliffs 1963, p. 33
118   "Peter Weiss zwischen den Ideologien," *Akzente* 12 (1965), p. 417

intended. He "rescues" them by a reluctance to represent "that which is not" which we have seen to be one of the most basic convictions of the young Brecht, and which remains with him to the end as a dismissal of all "false Utopias." "Wunschbilder des erfüllten Augenblicks" are few in his work; the pessimism, the insight we have observed at work in *Mahagonny* are too strong for that. As ever "Das Ziel lag in großer Ferne," that is, in mind and in hope.

CHAPTER THREE

Geh ich zeitig in die Leere
Komm ich aus der Leere voll.
Wenn ich mit dem Nichts verkehre
Weiß ich wieder, was ich soll.

Wenn ich liebe, wenn ich fühle
Ist es eben auch Verschleiß
Aber dann, in der Kühle
Werd ich wieder heiß.[1]

In this third and final chapter, I have endeavoured to show how the conclusions we have arrived at in our analysis of certain basic problems of Brecht's early work and of his first Marxist plays might be applied to a study of the later work, and what similarities and differences such an approach might reveal. For this purpose I have chosen a number of works from the later period, all of which seemed particularly fruitful for a demonstration of this kind. These interpretations do not in any sense aim at completeness — indeed, most of these works have already been the subject of a number of excellent critical studies — but rather at supplementing to some extent the more frequent approach through the theories and intentions of the later Brecht by an attempt to see the works themselves as a logical development of those factors we have seen to have been of such importance in his earlier work. The later plays and the later theories often seem to be regarded as a "canon," complete in themselves, and raising no questions they do not themselves answer; I have endeavoured to show that, for the present writer at least, this is not the case.

For this reason, I have decided against giving a detailed account of Brecht's later dramatic theory, a task which has already been performed more than adequately by others,[2] and have preferred to make use of his theoretical utterances only in so far as they are of direct relevance to the particular problems under consideration. The "positivity" of Brecht's theories, the somewhat idyllic character of the relation between theatre and society he proposes, for example, in the *Kleines Organon für das Theater*, can perhaps best be understood as a "projection of direction" of the kind we discussed in Chapter Two; the theories set up, in the theatre, the ideally rational kind of society whose continued absence in the world outside forms the harsh reality of Brecht's last years in East Berlin, yet the plays themselves, which are obliged to show the world as it is, and not as it ought to be, often tell a very different story. In the

---

[1] GW 10, p. 1024
[2] cf. esp. Walter Hinck, *Die Dramaturgie des späten Brecht*, Göttingen 1959, and Manfred Wekwerth, *Theater in Veränderung*, Berlin 1960

Kleines Organon Brecht seems to be describing the ideal theatre of an ideal society (perhaps under the influence of the initial optimism of his return to East Berlin); the tragic discrepancy between this "aesthetic" society and the real society in which he worked has been presented nowhere more clearly than in Günter Grass's controversial play, *Die Plebejer proben den Aufstand,* where Brecht (as "Der Chef"), despairing of the "real" revolution ever catching up with the "revolution" on stage, attempts bitterly to utilise the East Berlin rising for his own theatrical purposes, and to demonstrate by this means to the workers how far they are from the "true" revolutionary knowledge which might bring them success. So, also, an analysis of Brecht's "paradigm" for the theatre can tell us much of his intentions and desires, but often serves only to emphasise the distance between this ideal and the world of the works themselves.

I

Ich hatte als Wissenschaftler eine ein-
zigartige Möglichkeit. In meiner Zeit
erreichte die Astronomie die Markt-
plätze. Unter diesen ganz besonderen
Umständen hätte die Standhaftigkeit
eines Mannes große Erschütterungen
hervorrufen können. ... Ich habe zu-
dem die Überzeugung gewonnen, Sarti,
daß ich niemals in wirklicher Gefahr
schwebte. Einige Jahre lang war ich
ebenso stark wie die Obrigkeit. Und
ich überlieferte mein Wissen den
Machthabern, es zu gebrauchen, es
nicht zu gebrauchen, es zu miß-
brauchen, ganz wie es ihren Zwecken
diente.
Ich habe meinen Beruf verraten. Ein
Mensch, der das tut, was ich getan
habe, kann in den Reihen der Wissen-
schaft nicht geduldet werden.
Leben des Galilei, Schlußszene, 3. Fassung[3]

Any discussion of Brecht's later plays will almost inevitably begin and end with *Leben des Galilei.* Although finally far more conventional than *Der gute*

3 GW 3, p. 1341

Mensch von Sezuan and *Der kaukasische Kreidekreis* and somewhat atypical in its almost exclusive concentration on a dominant central character, the play continues to fascinate critics for two basic reasons: the unusual (and easily recognisable) degree of identification between author and protagonist, and the pronounced development in Brecht's attitude towards Galileo's recantation between the 1939 version and the final version of the play, on which he was still working in 1956.

Although the 1939 version has still not been published in full, it is easy to reconstruct the basic changes in Brecht's attitude from the evidence in Käthe Rülicke's excellent essay *Bemerkungen zur Schlußszene*[4] and the three scenes published by Gerhard Szczesny in 1966.[5] Galileo, who, in the first version, retells the "Keunergeschichte" *Maßnahmen gegen die Gewalt* in a thinly disguised form as a justification for his "new ethics" and whose Keunerian logic is finally recognised and approved by his strongest critic, Andrea, in the final scene, is condemned increasingly by Brecht in his revision of the play in 1955—1956 (indeed, the process continues beyond the published version of the play) as a traitor to science and its moral responsibility to the community. In a fragmentary note, Brecht traces this development back to the Californian version (1945) and comments unambiguously:

> In der kalifornischen Fassung (. . .) bricht Galilei die Lobeshymnen seines Schülers ab und beweist ihm, daß der Widerruf ein Verbrechen war und durch das Werk, so wichtig es sein mochte, nicht aufgewogen. Wenn es jemanden interessieren sollte: Dies ist auch das Urteil des Stückschreibers.[6]

The curiously oblique form of this final statement is echoed in another note on the 14th scene:

> Andrea Sartis Schlußbemerkung gibt keineswegs die Ansicht des Stückschreibers über Galilei wieder, sondern nur seine Ansicht über Andrea Sarti. Der Stückschreiber wünschte nicht das letzte Wort zu haben.[7]

This again, is an echo, this time of Andrea's own words in the final version: "Aber ich kann mir nicht denken, daß Ihre [Galileis] mörderische [Selbst-]Analyse das letzte Wort sein wird."[8]

Brecht's attitude, for all its apparent "Parteilichkeit," is strangely ambivalent. The "Stückschreiber" seems at one and the same time to affirm Galileo's self-accusations and yet to leave the door open for a "letztes Wort" which is neither Andrea's nor his own. This ambivalence becomes more readily

---

4 Now in *Materialien zu Brechts "Leben des Galilei,"* Frankfurt 1967, pp. 91ff.
5 Szczesny, op.cit., pp. 103ff.
6 GW 17, p. 1133
7 GW 17, p. 1132—3
8 GW 3, p. 1342

understandable if we assume, as there are many grounds for doing, that Galileo's self-condemnation is a self-condemnation by Bert Brecht, and that it is tempered by the hope that, perhaps, after all, "die Nachgeborenen" of whom he expects and requests "Nachsicht" for the weaknesses of the dark present, will judge more mildly.

Ernst Schuhmacher's thesis,[9] that from 1945 on *Galileo* was transformed into a play about the social responsibility of the scientist, does not stand up to close analysis. The parallel which Brecht saw in 1945 between Galileo's submission to the authority of the church and the situation of Oppenheimer and others is, in effect, an irrelevance. From the beginning, Brecht had seen in Galileo's "new science" not so much the emergence of a new technology, with its attendant dangers (since the *Badener Lehrstück* his attitude towards technological progress had been clearly sceptical), as the basis of a new "scientific logic," identical with Herr Keuner's "Wissen," which must lead to a total restructuring of society, as scene 9 (later 10) makes clear. This new logic, which Brecht appeals to again in the *Kleines Organon für das Theater* as a precise parallel to his own "Verfremdungstechnik," has explicit revolutionary overtones, and is imme- diately recognised for what it is by the common people:

> Der Maurer, der da ein Haus gebaut
> Der zieht nun selber ein
> Und der Holzhacker, der die Bäume haut,
> Schiebt das Holz in seinen eigenen Ofen rein.[10]

That Galileo should choose the anecdote *Maßnahmen gegen die Gewalt* to illustrate his reasons for remaining silent in scene 8 (which, after all, prefigure his reasons for renouncing his discoveries), merely proves to what extent he is practising this "new logic," in its related ethical form, in his own life: he is applying the results of Brecht's earlier *Keunergeschichten* with total conse- quence, and for the same reason as Herr Keuner; he is convinced, as a "Träger des Wissens," that this role is more important that any moral judgment that may be levelled against him, and his behaviour is certainly no more "treacherous" than that of "der Denkende" in *Die zwei Hergaben*. The dangerous gap between the discoveries of science and their application which Brecht saw in the play in 1945 is not allowed for by Galileo's own definition of science, as the "logic of the people" or "common sense." His key position in the history of Western science is due, for Brecht, not to the fact that his discoveries made modern technology possible, but to his revolt against the false logic of Aristotelean science, which parallelled Brecht's own revolt against the Aristotelean theatre

---

9 Ernst Schuhmacher, *Drama und Geschichte. Leben des Galilei und andere Stücke*, Berlin 1965
10 Szczesny, op.cit., p. 114

and which he saw as anticipating the final application of "common sense" to social relationships in the work of Karl Marx.

The attempt to superimpose a further "layer" on the logical structure of the first *Galileo* was thus from the beginning somewhat unfortunate, and Brecht's indecision in the Californian and Berlin versions as to whether Galileo is to be treated as a "historical figure" or as a "Modellfall," if it adds to the complexity of the issues, does not strengthen the unity of the argument. The inflation of the "Vanni" sub-plot, for instance, seems absurd and anachronistic on the historical level, while being too narrowly determined to have much "symbolic" force for the present (who are the scientists' "real allies" today?). The reader is not inclined to accept Galileo's own self-judgment for quite different reasons than Andrea's; his analysis of his own position of power at the height of his career seems absurdly inflated and quite unhistorical.

The reasons for this "inflation," however, are not hard to see, and stem from the dual functions that the Galileo of 1956 is required to fulfil. At one and the same time, his career is to be used as a "Modell" for a critique of Keunerian (Brechtian) "List," which will now concentrate, not on the results of this cunning, but on its dangers, and as a rather unsatisfactory "reading in the history of science," which ends up blaming poor old Galileo for the aberrations of the nuclear scientists of the twentieth century. The transparent unfairness of this second procedure only reveals to what extent it is a mask for Brecht's real pre-occupation in the play, whose strongly personal character clearly demanded such obliqueness. Brecht does not wish to have "das letzte Wort" on *Galileo* because, finally, it is he himself who is being judged.

This realisation might have rendered Szczesny's diatribes in his essay *Das Leben des Galilei und der Fall Bertolt Brecht* mercifully unnecessary, as the role of moral avenger which he assumes so fiercely has already been carried out by Brecht himself, to far greater effect. Equally, it is regrettable that Schuhmacher should find it necessary to go to the other extreme and reject Brecht's involvement in Galileo out of hand. The weakness of both approaches seems to lie in their inability to relate the first *Galileo* meaningfully to Brecht's preoccupations in the thirties and to see the later condemnation as, above all, an "Auseinandersetzung" with the conclusions of the earlier work, rather than with the problem of the social responsibility of the scientist.

Brecht's increasing dissatisfaction with Herr Keuner's "logic of survival" is by no means, as we shall see, merely a product of the trauma of 1953, although the East Berlin uprising may well have proved, in many ways, a last straw. Throughout the late plays and poems, one can trace an increasing realisation that survival is not enough, that the problem of who or what is to survive must also be solved, and not merely "ausgespart," as it had been in the early *Lehrstücke*. Shen Te's dilemma, "gut zu sein und doch zu leben" is now posed with a seriousness which stands in striking contrast to the cynical solutions Brecht had advanced to it in his early work; survival is useless if the qualities which will make life worthwhile "after the flood" are destroyed in the process. Herr Keuner's logic, as we have seen, is too easy a way out; sooner or later, Herr Egge will have to make use of his "nein," to acquire a "Rückgrat," or else his "List" may serve only to prolong the exile of "Niemandsein."

Even at the time of its composition, the first version of *Galileo* was only one of Brecht's answers to the problem. The two "Kalendergeschichten" *Der Mantel des Ketzers*[11] and *Das Experiment*[12] seem to present the two extremes between which Galileo's argument is to vacillate. Giordano Bruno is the ideal "new scientist," whose new insight into the solar system is matched by his understanding of the tailor's wife and her very real problems; yet his faithfulness to his new ideas leads him to the "Scheiterhaufen." Francis Bacon, on the other hand, is even more of a flawed personality than Galileo, a man "der nicht wenige seiner Zeigenossen mit Abscheu erfüllt hatte, aber auch viele mit Begeisterung für die nützlichen Wissenschaften."[13] Like Galileo, he is allowed, on the point of death, to pass on his knowledge to an uncorrupted "youth" who will transmit it to future generations. While in *Der Mantel des Ketzers* Brecht does not hesitate to idealise Bruno in a manner somewhat unusual in his work (to some extent, the characterisation of the tailor's wife, who is the centre of interest in the story, demands it as a foil), he abstains from any jugment on the relationship between Bacon's political career and his scientific discoveries, presenting it as an unexplained contradiction. Here again, the problem of communication seems more important than that of moral judgment.

There is every evidence that it was a problem that pre-occupied Brecht in these years, and it has left definite traces in the first *Galileo*. Galileo's parting words to Andrea in the first version, "Nimm dich in acht, wenn du durch Deutschland fährst und die Wahrheit unter dem Rock trägst"[14] have, as has been pointed out, a direct significance they lack in the later versions; they might almost have been taken word for word from the essay *Fünf Schwierigkeiten beim Schreiben der Wahrheit,*[15] which was itself "smuggled" into Germany. There is no clear distinction máde between the truths that Galileo has discovered and the truths that Bert Brecht wishes to communicate to the German people, and indeed, Galileo's enforced isolation is a distorted image of Brecht's own in the days of emigration. Laotse, as we shall see, faces a similar problem; his knowledge is only communicated by chance, as he is on the point of leaving the country.

---

11 GW 11, pp. 276ff.
12 GW 11, pp. 264ff.
13 GW 11, p. 275
14 Szczesny, p. 128
15 GW 18, pp. 222ff.

Two problems obviously arise, both central to a discussion of the later
Brecht; what happens if this communication does not take place, if the bearer of
knowledge is never able to transfer it, and to what extent is the communication
of knowledge a moral category which overrides all others? The first problem
had a particular relevance for Brecht in emigration, where the audience to whom
he spoke seemed deaf or inaccessible, but it lies too, as we have seen, behind the
opposition "Unwissende! schrie ich / Schuldbewußt" of the late poem *Böser
Morgen,* which is the self-accusation of the teacher who has not passed on his
knowledge to those who need it. The second problem becomes increasingly
dominant, to the point where Galileo can be summarily dismissed by his creator
and *alter ego,* Bert Brecht, as a "Verbrecher."

What explains the violence of this final rejection? It is difficult to resist
the temptation to see in it Brecht's own castigation of the too successful logic of
survival he practised on the 17th June, 1953; without wishing to be as
doctrinaire as Esslin, one cannot really avoid the impression that the *Buckower
Elegien* and the attack on *Galileo* stand in some relation to the events of 1953,
which Brecht was not allowed to forget by his Western friends. The
Schweijk-like aptitude for "Überleben" that Brecht was so proud of and which
gave rise to so many of the legends and anecdotes about him was bound, sooner
or later, to come into conflict with the moral issue of valid protest, an issue
which, for all Brecht's cleverness, had not been resolved in the early *Lehrstücke*
and the *Keunergeschichten.* Kattrin's "protest" in *Mutter Courage* is in many
ways the most effective critique of Galileo's cunning; like Grusche, she is not
clever enough to stifle her basic reactions, and so sucumbs to the good. However
much Brecht seeks to relativise her action and Grusche's, by pointing out its
untenability and the limitations of understanding which lead to it, he succeeds
only in amassing arguments against his own earlier standpoint, that "Hilfe" must
be eliminated until the storm of "Gewalt" is over and past; the retreat into the
elephant-hide of Herr Keuner can only be a temporary solution, and, for all its
class justification, it remains fraught with danger, not least the danger of being
revealed as a cover for naked self-interest or self-indulgence. It is this criticism
that the late Galileo is made to bear the brunt of, as a stand-in for Bert Brecht,
who had developed too great a skill at assuming his "kleinste Größe" to abandon
it where necessary. It is perhaps neither Brecht's own "letztes Wort," nor his
reader's, yet it marks a significant rejection of the strategy by which he had
survived the crisis of the late twenties and shows clearly the extent to which the
later work has moved away from the "extinction of the individual" from which
it began.

In the first version of *Galileo* Brecht summons up all his optimism to allow
Galileo in his last words to Andrea a renewed affirmation of belief in "die neue
Zeit," brave words in 1939. In the final version, this has been pared down to a
mere "Doch" in answer to Andrea's question. The "neue Zeit" many arrive for

Andrea, but Galileo has disqualified himself from participating in it. To repeat Klaus Heinrich's words:

> Herr K. [Galileo!] hat die Schwierigkeiten des Niemand nicht gelöst. Er hat sie erläutert und dadurch sich als Identität kenntlich gemacht. Es ist sehr fraglich, ob er schon der "Denkende" war, der "in seiner kleinsten Größe" den Sturm übersteht.[16]

II

> Die Zuschauer bei Katastrophen erwarten ja zu Unrecht, daß die Betroffenen daraus lernen werden. Solange die Masse das Objekt der Politik ist, kann sie, was mit ihr geschieht, nicht als einen Versuch, sondern nur als ein Schicksal ansehen; sie lernt so wenig aus der Katastrophe wie das Versuchskarnickel über Biologie lernt. Dem Stückschreiber obliegt es nicht, die Courage am Ende sehend zu machen — sie sieht einiges, gegen die Mitte des Stückes zu, am Ende der sechsten Szene, und verliert dann die Sicht wieder —, ihm kommt es darauf an, daß der Zuschauer sieht.
>
> Anmerkung zu *Mutter Courage* (1949)[17]

From its first performance in Zürich on 19th April, 1941, *Mutter Courage* has been the subject of much controversy. Generally accepted as Brecht's "masterpiece," it has been the subject of most of the attempts to relate the "theory" to the "practice," to compare Brecht's expressed intentions with the "result" in his literary work. It is perhaps unfortunate that *Courage* should have been singled out for this treatment, which might have shown better results elsewhere, for instance with *Der gute Mensch von Sezuan*, for *Mutter Courage* is not a play of "decisions" in the sense that so many of Brecht's other plays, beginning from *Die heilige Johanna der Schlachthöfe*, are, nor is it a play of "development." There is no substantial change in the character and insight of Courage

---

16 Heinrich, op.cit., p. 56
17 GW 17, p. 1150

throughout the play — her "moment of insight" ("sie sieht einiges") is not a point towards which her character develops. It is, as Brecht takes care to emphasise, in the scheme of things more of an "accident." Her momentary rejection of the war seems almost incidental, since there are so many other points in the play where she seems to have grounds for such a rejection, and yet fails to see. Brecht's thesis in 1949 is that, like the "Versuchskarnickel" of the quotation, she is unable to learn from experience; for her, the perpetual catastrophe which surrounds her is "Schicksal," she can see no alternative to the course of action she has chosen.

Once again, the difficulties of an interpretation of *Mutter Courage* seem to spring largely from a change in the conception of the heroine's character in the years which lie between its composition in 1939 and its production in East Berlin in 1948–49. This production marked the founding of the Berliner Ensemble; it was also Brecht's first "appearance" in the German Democratic Republic. The play was obliged to fulfil a new function in keeping with the new environment in which it was performed.

Again, we cannot ignore the organic way in which the *Courage* of 1939 fits into the development of Brecht's theory of "survival." It stands in a complex relationship to the first *Galilei,* where Galileo's survival, even at the cost of his renunciation, is still "worth-while," because he manages to rescue his "Wissen" and preserve the right to work. Courage is a far more ambivalent character, and this ambivalence seems to be inherent in her characterisation and not simply a result of Brecht's changing attitude to her; she is at once Lao Tse and the "Zöllner," both the teacher and the potential pupil. Throughout the play, it is Courage who sees things most clearly, whose Keuner-like descriptions of the war and the society which produces it strike us with their aptness, and yet she is at the same time the "victim" of this society, unable to rise above it, unable to convert her "insight" into anything more than a stoic scepticism. Unlike Johanna, she is by no means a "simple soul" who is destroyed by her guilelessness — there is, in fact, no decision for her to make. As Brecht writes in *Die Dialektik auf dem Theater* in 1951:

> Die dem Publikum tief fühlbare Tragik der Courage und ihres Lebens bestand darin, daß hier ein entsetzlicher Widerspruch bestand, der einen Menschen vernichtete, ein Widerspruch, der gelöst werden konnte, aber nur von der Gesellschaft selbst, und in langen, schrecklichen Kämpfen.[18]

For Courage the war is "Schicksal," because as an individual she is presented with no possible alternative to her course of action. There is no "right" decision to make, as there is in the world of *Johanna;* in fact, Courage has more skill at surviving in this world than most of the others, like Galileo she is a strong figure rather than a weak one, one who has learnt a great deal from the tactics of Herr Keuner. But in this society no-one can win, not even Tilly. The situation of the play lacks the "special" quality of *Johanna;* Courage is presented not with a crisis, with a special development which demands action of her and shows her how to act, but with a "state" which she seems to have no hope of changing. At least a part of Brecht's "Verfremdung" is designed to demonstrate the essential sameness of war and peace (as in the equation of the *Dreigroschenroman,* "Bürger=Räuber"). He sees the war as a logical development of capitalism, as a pursual of its aims with other means, and one of the most persistent sources of irony in the play is the application of the vocabulary of peace to war and of war to peace. In *Mutter Courage,* too, there is no "opposition" to the war, which is accepted, more or less without complaint, as a way of life and death which it is useless to protest against and which has lasted as long as living memory; the proletariat of *Johanna* is silent.

Johanna is set in a "Chicago" contemporary to the action of the play, distorted of course beyond recognition, but in the direction, as with *Mahagonny,* of a wider recognition — as a "Modell" for the contemporary world. *Mutter Courage* is set in the Germany of the Thirty Years' War. Like the majority of the later plays, it is removed by a wide space (either temporally or geographically) from the world of the present. In *Johanna,* the application of the play to the problems of its "present," as we have seen, is immediately apparent; in *Courage,* on the other hand, it is far more oblique. The world of *Courage* represents an early stage of the historical dialectic, where it is impossible for Courage, however hard she tries, to achieve the "insight" which Brecht demands that the audience should deduce from her predicament: it is simply not available to her. To desert the war, to attempt to survive as a peasant, seems no better a solution for her (compare the "Wer in seinem Kober blieb" of *Mahagonny*), as the play itself demonstrates clearly enough. Courage's shrewdness allows her at least to delay the inevitable disaster — she may have little "insight," but the others have less. Her attempt "an dem Krieg ihren Schnitt zu machen" is merely the attempt to survive in a society which *is* the war, and her "tragedy" is that, while her methods ensure her own survival as surely as Herr Egge's his, her children, on whom she is dependent, are unable to emulate her shrewdness. Courage is determined to survive, even if it means reducing herself to her "kleinste Größe," but her children expose themselves to the "storm" by their "virtues," like the early Brechtian heroes: Eilif, like Jimmy Mahony, is destroyed by the anarchy which his own "bravery" summons up, Schweizerkas, like Galy Gay, falls victim to his own simple nature, Kattrin stands almost at the opposite pole to Courage in her naive "Menschlichkeit," which has something of Johanna in it and something of Shen Te. It is Courage who follows the commandment of the *Badener Lehrstück;* her gradual ruin is only the gradual ruin of those around her.

Her plight at the end is certainly pathetic, but most of all because the value of her survival is being called in question; her tactics have been useless.

That Courage's survival is "sinnlos" seems in 1939 to be less an object-lesson for the audience than an expression of Brecht's own hopelessness at the time, a pessimism which in 1948 required correction. The "split" in Courage's personality, the strange combination of wisdom and foolishness which Brecht attempts to demonstrate in her character in 1948, is the result of an increasing rejection of Courage's solution to the problem of survival, which makes it necessary for Brecht to convert an on the whole "sympathetic" character, like the early Galileo, into an increasingly negative one. Yet both Galileo and Mutter Courage share too many of the features of Herr Keuner, of Brecht himself, for their "special pleading" to allow of an easy conversion, and their origin belies them. The kind of optimism which Brecht was later to achieve in *Der kaukasische Kreidekreis* is impossible in 1939, where an optimism of any kind was difficult enough. The Hitler—Stalin pact can have been a no easier pill for Brecht to swallow than for other German Communists, even if it shows some of the signs of a Keunerian logic itself. This is the period of "An die Nachgeborenen," where the "flood" is preparing to break over the world and destroy Herr Keuner with the rest of humanity. Brecht is left only with a metaphysical hope that a new humanity will succeed the general destruction and carry on the knowledge which has been "aufgegeben" by their predecessors.

Yet if *Mutter Courage* seems a "pessimistic" play, it is by no means because Brecht "renounces" Marxism in any way, but because it is the work in which he expresses most clearly and most independently the pessimism which, for him, is the "reason" for his Marxism, which gives his eventual optimism its "true" quality, and in 1948 Brecht expects the audience to add this dimension to the work. In 1939 *Courage* was not designed as an exhortation to Marxist optimism — which at that date must have seemed hopelessly unrealistic — but as an expose of the futility and hopelessness of war and of a society which is built on a system which allows war, and it is as such that we still experience the play. It is a different matter to "deduce" optimism from this pessimism. We must ask ourselves what evidence the play provides us with for such a deduction.

In the 1949 *Anmerkung* Brecht deplores the effect of the Zürich premiere, "trotz der antifaschistischen und pazifistischen Einstellung des hauptsächlich von deutschen Emigranten besetzten Schauspielhauses."[19] Even in this formulation the contradiction seems to be inherent which characterises so many of Brecht's later utterances on *Courage* and provoked a good deal of official criticism in East Germany: Brecht's failure to distinguish between "pacifists" and "anti-fascists." A "pacifist," for instance, could see little else but tragedy in *Mutter Courage,* as he himself would have no means of changing the society

---

[19] *Stücke* 7, pp. 205ff. I have been unable to locate this passage in the *Werkausgabe.*

whose victim she is; an "antifascist," by Brecht's own definition of the thirties, must meet "Gewalt" with "Gewalt," and might learn from the failure of Courage's passivity. But we have already seen that *Courage* differs greatly from *Johanna* in that it does not provide the audience with any other reason for changing the world by force than the intolerability of the situation, it does not attempt to convince them that there are grounds for hope, that the world can be changed. Thus *Courage* is placed in the strange position of providing its "true" solution only to one who is already convinced, who like Brecht is able to "carry" the pessimism of the play in his own optimism. The "bourgeois" critics who called *Courage* a "Niobe-tragedy"[20] were of course misled, but it is important to consider why, to analyse the "effect" of the play and not only the "intention," which we have seen to have in any case something of the character of a later attempt at "Umfunktionieren" about it. Brecht was "warned" by this reaction: of the lack of explicit direction of his play, certainly, and of the need to "estrange" the audience's sympathy somewhat from Courage in order that they should not identify themselves too closely with her fate; but also at a more private level. Courage has failed to make herself "unkenntlich": she becomes a tragic figure because she does not succeed in becoming "niemand." Instead of seeing in her the representative of a class or of a period we see her as an individual, who like Herr Keuner knows of the difficulties of survival and makes herself "behaftbar" by her talk of them, so that in the end we remain preoccupied with the difficulties of the individual rather than the eventual triumph of the "class." She is not a conventional "heroine," but the sympathy which she obtains and must obtain, and which, despite all attempts to the contrary, Brecht never succeeded in eliminating from his own production — Courage's new "negative" traits only stress the difficulty with which she survives, the impossibility "gut zu sein und doch zu leben" — militates against the kind of "disappearance" which is expected of her at the end. Like Chaplin's characters she belongs to the class of the "plebeian heroes" whose heroism consists in surviving the "finstere Zeiten" of history, and we cannot help sympathising with her plight and the "courage" with which she endures it, even if this courage is dictated by the will to survive.

What is the "Zuschauer" to see, to deduce from *Mutter Courage?* Surely, that a world in which "virtue" leads to destruction, where survival has no meaning, where there is no "Ausweg" (compare "Der Nachgeborene"), must be changed. The war and the society which is responsible for it must be "abgeschafft." It is intolerable that people should be forced to die like Eilif, Schweizerkas and Kattrin, or to live like Courage. Yet the play itself provides us with no vision of a better world, nor with any means of attaining it. We are not

20 loc.cit.

shown how the new society is to rise above the "flood"; Brecht can show us only the "Auslöschung" of the old society, with good and bad, who are both unable to assert themselves against it. For the "Zuschauer," optimism is not the "natural" conclusion, Courage is, like the "Zöllner" in *Legende von der Entstehung des Buches Taoteking auf dem Weg des Laotse in die Emigration,* "kein Sieger"; moreover, there is no Laotse to tell her that ". . . das weiche Wasser in Bewegung / mit der Zeit den mächtigen Stein besiegt."[21] It is hard to see the "rulers of tommorrow" in the oppressed of the Thirty Years' War as Brecht shows them in *Mutter Courage.*[22]

We have seen that the world of *Mahagonny* presents a kind of perspective of contemporary society, distorted to bring out its true character; in the same way, the "Chicago" of *Johanna* is used to project the crisis with which Brecht and his audience are faced more clearly onto the confusion that surrounds them. In what relation, then, does the world of the Thirty Years' War stand to the reality of its "present?" In 1948, Brecht attempts to minimise this relationship, to suggest that the "Courage of today" is in a different situation, that she, unlike the heroine of the play, does have an alternative, a "way out." But the play itself seems not only to fail to produce such an alternative, it seems actually to discount the possibility of one, by its failure to include the "grounds for optimism." We have seen that such an alternative is ruled out both by the actual historical setting of the play and by the contingencies of the time at which it was originally written. There seems, however, to be an even more basic problem involved — the whole problem of writing a "historical" play which deals with pre-Marxist times and yet implies a "Marxist" conclusion.

The final effect of *Mutter Courage* is bound up to a very large extent with the essential difficulties involved in Brecht's use of a historical setting which cannot easily be related to the contingencies of a "decision" to embrace the "historical mission" of Marxism. In the later *Galilei,* we are embarrassed by Brecht's argument that Galileo has under-estimated his strength, which seems an anachronism designed to make the application of the play more clear; in *Courage* the complete lack of a mechanism designed to show that three hundred years are "keine Kleinigkeit" (to paraphrase Piscator's comment on the effect of his production of *Die Räuber*[23]) leads us to see the world of the Thirty Years' War not as the past, but as the present, as a perspective of the world of 1939 in the same way that *Mahagonny* is a perspective of the world of 1929, and there is no doubt that it is at least partly intended in this sense. But if the world of *Courage* comes to be taken entirely as the world of today, and the "historical" quality of its setting becomes merely incidental, then Brecht's failure to present Courage

21 GW 9, p. 661
22 cf. GW 9, p. 752. I wonder if there is any significance in the fact that this poem is suddenly thought to be much earlier than on its first publication? (*Gedichte* 8, p. 183)
23 cf. GW 15, p. 112

with an alternative becomes a failure to suggest one for the present. The Thirty Years' War with its untold sufferings and its disastrous aftermath becomes an image of the twentieth century, rather than a stage which has been left behind.

This danger seem to be inherent in the whole process of "Historisierung." The fondness of the twentieth century for satirising the past by presenting it "in modern dress" may have its origins in the burlesque of the eighteenth century — a tradition which is preserved in the revue-sketch of today — but it emerges with the work of Shaw in particular on a new and more serious level. His St. Joan, his Androcles, speak the language of the twentieth century drawing room — historical personages are shown to be people "like you and me," and the problems of yesterday are equated, often superficially, with the problems of today. History comes to be seen as "ewiges, geschichtsloses Hier und Jetzt"[24] — all historical times are one, the problems of human "nature" remain the same. This problem is not merely restricted to the drama — Hans Mayer sees it as a central characteristic of the work of Gottfried Benn,[25] it appears too in Rilke as the "simultaneity" of past and present in Malte's world. Whether the end effect is comic or tragic — Friedrich Dürrenmatt has seen perhaps more clearly than anyone the essential irrelevance of these terms to contemporary literature[26] — it is always the "present" which remains, the level of the performers, which imposes itself on the past and re-interprets the past in terms of the present. Caesar, Moses, Don Juan, Galileo all belong to the same age and speak the same language. This is a basically different approach from the histories of earlier periods, for whom the past was either classical Greece or Rome, the epitome of all culture, or the "primitive stages of the present," as in Shakespeare's histories, both "distanced" from the present by the highly formalised language of tragedy. The conversational prose of the modern "history" has the opposite effect — instead of distancing the action from us, it makes it part of our present — we tend to justify the comparison which is implicit between past and present, to say: perhaps Caesar did think like that, perhaps Rome was after all not so different from Berlin, perhaps we are in the same kind of situation as Courage. The plays become a new kind of popular "Geschichtsschreibung," and indeed, this is their source: they stem from a rejection of the history of the history books (compare Brecht's poem "Fragen eines lesenden Arbeiters"[27]), a dissatisfaction which the twentieth century feels with the impersonal motivation of the great of history, a depreciation of the tragic hero. Much of this "re-writing" of history is primarily satiric; Dürrenmatt's analysis of late Roman society in Romulus der Große combines an irresistibly "comic" debunking of the traditional version of the fall of the Roman Empire with a carefully executed

24 Hans Mayer, Bertolt Brecht und die Tradition, p. 12
25 loc.cit.
26 cf. Theaterprobleme, Zurich 1955, pp. 42ff.
27 GW 9, p. 656

satire of European society after the war which gains at least some of its impetus from the plausibility of the comparison.

In *Mutter Courage,* however, there is no "satire" to point the duality of past and present; such satire as there is is directed not at the "present in the past," but at the "whole" of past and present. The two periods do not throw one another into relief, but stress rather the "timelessness," the universality of the state which is common to both of them, just as Sartre's *Les Mouches* the transposition of the theme into Ancient Greece emphasises the timless nature of Orestes' predicament. The two periods do not "sich gegenseitig verfremden" — the world of *Courage* seems a "Modell" for the present-day world in the same sense as Mahagonny. The danger of such a stylisation we have already seen with reference to *Die Dreigroschenoper,* which provoked Tucholsky to the expression "stilisiertes Bayern";[28] is not *Mutter Courage* in a similar way a "stylised" image of the present day? The devices Brecht uses in *Der gute Mensch von Sezuan* to prevent such a simple equivalence are missing here (complex levels of speech, "unreal" elements, alienating commentary); even the songs are fitted more closely to the demands of the plot than is usual in Brecht.

In a recent article Hans Mayer compares the "open endings" of Peter Weiss's play *Die Verfolgung und Ermordung Jean Paul Marats dargestellt durch die Schauspielgruppe des Hospizes zu Charenton unter Anleitung des Herrn Sade* and of *Der gute Mensch von Sezuan* and arrives at the conclusion that, while the "openness" of Weiss's play is genuine, in Brecht's it is merely "gespielt."[29] This seems to the present writer a quite erroneous conclusion: it implies that Brecht could have and would have presented the "conclusion" which is to be drawn from the play in the play itself, if he had so wished, but that, as a compliment to the intelligence of his audience, he omits it and leaves them to supply it for themselves, just as Professor Mayer's students provided the "missing" verse of the "Schneider von Ulm."[30] But surely our position with regard to these two works is somewhat different; men have learnt to fly, but Shen Te's problem has not been solved; indeed, Brecht seems to imply that only a partial and gradual solution is possible. We may assume that a knowledge of Marxism is a useful prerequisite for the audience of Brecht's plays, and even that a convinced Marxist may achieve a special understanding of them, but we can scarcely elevate the "achieving" of socialism to a *conditio sine qua non* for this audience. One imagines that few enough Marxists would support so trite an analogy as that between flying and the eventual solution of the moral problem of achieving a just society. Mayer seems to be confusing intention and result.

---

[28] *Dreigroschenbuch*, p. 218
[29] "Berliner Dramaturgie von Gerhart Hauptmann bis Peter Weiss," *Theater heute* 12 (1965), pp. 1ff., cf. esp. p. 7.
[30] cf. Mayer, *Ansichten*, Hamburg 1962, p. 110–11

No one doubts Brecht's desire to deduce the necessity of Marxism from his work, but on the other hand his literary work never succeeds in demonstrating more than the need for a change, the intolerability of the present. Brecht is prepared to commit himself neither on the question of whether the new society will, in fact, be able to achieve its ends, nor on how it is to achieve them. *Mutter Courage* is the most negative of all the late plays, in that it seems to leave these questions not merely unanswered, but even unasked. If we were to assume the classical "cultured Persian gentleman" as audience, he, not having so much as heard of Marxism, might be moved by the play to demand a change, but he would be at a loss to give more than a vague idea of the direction which the author seemed to be proposing. Yet one must deny that these "open endings" are the result of calculation on Brecht's part, that they represent a little aesthetic trick designed to send the audience home murmuring delightedly, "Ah! we knew it all the time, her mistake was in not living in the Twentieth Century and joining the Party" — Brecht denies the possibility of Marxism to his characters for far more valid reasons. The openness of his plots is an expression of the consciousness we have already seen formulated in *Irrtum und Fortschritt:* "Nur so verhindert man, daß etwas fertig wird."[31] Their problems have not been solved, a solution may be in progress of being achieved, but to close the play now is to say (to borrow an expression from the language of the Houyhnhmns) "the thing which is not," to give up the hope of the future for the "mistakes" of the present. Just as Marx and Engels deduced the necessity of Marxism from the analysis of history and in particular, of their own time, so Brecht endeavours to reproduce in his plays the analysis which leads him to believe in this infinite dialectic of progress, rather than an uncertain and ultimately "untrue" Utopia in the future; he presents the "groundwork" rather than the conclusion itself. Himself sufficiently aware of the difficulty of reaching and supporting such a conclusion, and of its "hypothetical" character, he presents rather the "insight" into society he has gained which leads him to believe in the necessity of such a change. The "mistakes" of the present, like the mistakes of Herr Keuner, become positive within the context of the dialectic that carries them. Even the second "Hergabe" may be the anticipation of a new synthesis. "Error," like Mephistopheles in *Faust I,* becomes a positive force in that it aids the "good" in its development and prevents stasis. As Brecht was later to write in a newspaper article:

Kein neuer Staat kann aufgebaut werden ohne Zuversicht; es ist der Überschuß an Kraft, der die neue Gesellschaft baut. Aber ein oberflächlicher Optimismus kann sie in Gefahr bringen . . . Schönfärberei und Beschönigung

---

31 GW 12, p. 401

sind nicht nur die ärgsten Feinde der Schönheit, sondern auch der politischen Vernunft.[32]

To provide a falsely optimistic conclusion is to destroy the true nature of the argument, which relies on a precise and realistic representation of the evidence. On the level of the work itself, this is joined with a conviction that the "true" is also the beautiful, that "realism" is in fact the most important of all criteria. For Brecht, a socialist art which ignores this criterion to present "Utopia" on stage, to provide solutions to all questions, is "Kitsch." As we have already seen, this conviction of the necessity of a "total realism" is from the very beginning one of Brecht's most basic principles, and his criticism of the "false optimism" of socialist realism is substantially the same criticism that he had been making since Augsburg of literature which failed to "tell the truth" about the world. The "Utopian" has no place in his work because it cannot be expressed in terms of the existing society; it remains "outside" the work as a kind of unattainable limit which gives it direction.

Again, this is a very delicately balanced construction. In the later work it seems often to come into mild conflict with Brecht's personal need to be convinced not merely of the "rightness" of the "system" but of the "stage" itself. We have seen how his dialectic allows for a phase which is almost wholly negative, the phase of *Die zwei Hergaben* and of *Mutter Courage;* yet Brecht seems to become increasingly concerned that this stage should not in fact assume the character of an "end," that Herr Keuner's knowledge should not in fact be lost for ever. The tiredness, the despair of "An die Nachgeborenen" that the "goal" is so far away that all human values must perish in the meantime leads in *Der kaukasische Kreidekreis* to a strange kind of impatience to present a "temporary" solution, while at the same time insisting on its exceptional character. The same attitude seems to be at work in the 1948 production of *Courage;* the "negative" character of the phase represented begins to worry Brecht himself and he attempts to "de-universalise" it. The "pessimistic" antithesis of his "second optimism" threatens to engulf the thesis, or at least to force it out of the present, to allow the possibility of optimism only after a long negative phase in which the author is "fated" to live. Indeed, in some of the last poems there is a hint of an even more basic pessimism, a fear that the "new society" may never arise from the "flood," that the "good" may perish in the world.

Mutter Courage is, in many ways, a transitional figure, and like all Brecht's transitional figures, she was "rethought" by him. She is, in fact, the first expression of the rejection of "mere survival" which is so apparent in *Der gute Mensch von Sezuan* and *Der kaukasische Kreidekreis*. The first *Galilei,* while

---

32 GW 19, p. 541

endorsing Galileo's strategy, prepares the way for this questioning by its sharper formulation of the issue: the qualities which in Galileo were still positive have become negative in her. Courage's "wisdom" is of the same kind as Galileo's — she is equipped by Brecht with all the attributes of a healthy realism typical of his later heroes. Her "failure" is the same failure, essentially, as that of the later Galileo; in her concern for survival she forgets the purpose of survival. Yet there seems little doubt that Brecht's attitude to this "failure" has changed by 1948; his representation of Courage as "eine Hyäne des Krieges" seems to run contrary to the bulk of the text itself, which shows her as a wise woman who has to act against her inclinations in order to "make her way," just as Shui Ta is obliged to do things which for Shen Te are impossible. Brecht shows the same sympathy for Courage that Giordano Bruno feels for the tailor's wife in *Der Mantel des Ketzers;* he understands the struggle for survival which lies behind the apparent harshness of her actions. The reality of *Courage* remains the reality of 1939, a reality where even Herr Keuner can only survive in his anonymity in the hope that somebody will one day "demand" his wisdom of him, before like Laotse he "leaves the country" for good. There were few "ways out" for Brecht himself; the ambiguous position of the Soviet Union (Brecht was in a position to know of the effects of the Great Purge and of the delicate status of German Communists in Russia), the "inevitable" advance of Nazism, his exposed position in Scandinavia and the prospect of an America which was for him no "promised land," all contributed to a situation which seemed to offer little ground for optimism. It is, in the circumstances, not surprising that Courage does not "see" and we can scarcely be blamed if for us the "pessimism" of the play remains its final statement, since the "optimism" which would re-direct it lies outside the play itself.

III

The pessimistic "Gegenpol" of Brecht's optimism in these years is perhaps nowhere more directly expressed, and explained, than in two of the most "personal" poems of the *Svendborger Gedichte* (1933–1939) to which we have already had much occasion to refer: "An die Nachgeborenen" and "Legende von der Entstehung des Buches Taoteking auf dem Weg des Laotse in die Emigration."[33] Of these, the first is a "confessional" poem of a kind which had become rare in Brecht's output since 1929 — in many ways it seems an "answer" to the earlier "Vom armen B. B.," an extension and correction of the earlier poem — whereas in the second Brecht characterises his position in terms of another *alter ego* of these years, the philosopher Laotse. Both poems express a

[33] GW 9, p. 722, p. 660

weariness, a consciousness of the "hopelessness" of the present, against which they set the hope that "one day" (compare the "Sankt Nimmerleinstag" of *Der gute Mensch von Sezuan*[34]) the good may triumph, the cause of the just which is so pitifully weak and so lacking in appearance of success may prevail.

Laotse, like Brecht, is forced to leave the country where his "work" lies to take refuge in an anonymous emigration; the country to which he flees is, in fact, so vague that this emigration becomes almost a "death," as the second "Hergabe" is, in fact, really a death for "der Denkende" in *Die zwei Hergaben*. He is "gebrechlich," unable to continue the fight against the "evil" which is all too dominant in his country, where his protest, like Herr Egge's, remains unheard, useless, so that he prefers rather to retire into anonymity and "Ruh" to wait the turning of history. With his few wants (again a Brechtian trait, common to these poems of emigration), he leaves the "valley" and sets out into the mountains. We are immediately reminded of an aphorism of Brecht's on his return to Germany:

> Die Mühen der Gebirge liegen hinter uns
> Vor uns liegen die Mühen der Ebenen.[35]

Laotse is in no hurry to cross these "mountains of emigration": "Denn dem ging es schnell genug." Like the Brecht of "Der Radwechsel,"[36] "er ist nicht gern, wo er herkommt, er ist nicht gern, wo er hinfährt." He has little to look forward to. For the "teacher," life is not easy — he has no "Kostbarkeiten zu verzollen." But then Laotse's "Wissen" is preserved after all, almost by mistake. Out of politeness and curiosity, the customs official asks what he has found out in his studies, and is suddenly moved by the sentence about water and rock, with its image of hope, to ask him to write it down before he disappears behind the black fir-tree (which seems here to have the function of a death-symbol). There is some irony in the knowledge that the first sentence that Laotse will write has been translated as "The way that can be told is not the constant way,"[37] a truly Keunerian remark, yet Laotse, like Herr Keuner, is prepared to make the attempt, to provide some temporary, perhaps mistaken, hypotheses of the "way." For in the image of water and rock is contained the possibility that the official and others like him, oppressed and poverty-stricken and themselves not "conquerors" may, like the water, in time wear down the "rock" of injustice, however permanent and "fate-like" it may seem. And so he communicates his hope — and it is little more than that — before finally disappearing behind the "black fir." The poem ends, however, with an exhortation not to overlook the role of the official in the preservation of this wisdom, which without his action

34   GW 4, pp. 1562–3
35   GW 10, p. 960
36   GW 10, p. 1009
37   cf. Lao Tzu, *Tao Te Ching*, tr. D. C. Lau, Harmondsworth 1963, p. 57

would have been lost, a risk which we have seen to threaten Herr Keuner's
wisdom as well. We can perhaps best understand this concern with the survival of
the truth (and for Brecht, "Die Wahrheit ist konkret") by a brief comparison
with the poem which follows in the *Svendborger Gedichte,* "Besuch bei den
verbannten Dichtern,"[38] where Brecht conjurs up a vision of the "nameless"
poets whose work has been suppressed altogether and whose "message"lost.
Even Galileo is only able to save his "Discorsi" from oblivion by chance; he owes
their survival to an unexpected visit from Andrea. The "strategy" of Herr
Keuner becomes meaningless if there is no-one to receive the "knowledge"
which is the sole justification of his existence as "teacher."

"Die Mühen der Gebirge" are even more extreme in "An die Nachgeborenen,"
which shows its concern for survival, for "posterity," in the title itself, with its
direct appeal to those who will one day have emerged from the holocaust of the
present into a new and calmer world. Again, we have an attempt to justify the
hopelessness of the present by reference to a future where the "impossible" has
happened, where "das Unerreichbare" has become "das noch nicht Erreichte"
and it again seems possible to progress towards it.

The "finstere Zeiten" of the first part of the poem form the background
against which *Mutter Courage* and *Der gute Mensch von Sezuan* are set; in
particular, their closeness to the world of the later plays is apparent, and reflects
itself in a similarity of language and style to Shen Te's own monologues. It is a
world where survival can only be achieved at the cost of others, where the
"simple pleasures" of life, eating, drinking, laughing, "talking about trees," have
become almost a "crime" because they imply a forgetting of the state of
perpetual crisis which surrounds the poet. "Wisdom" itself is no longer possible,
since the world demands of the wise man that he forsake his wisdom, his
"distance," and himself help to rectify the intolerable state of affairs. The
simplest humanity will not allow him to detach himself from what is going on:
"Eine glatte Stirn / Deutet auf Unempfindlichkeit hin." Like Shen Te, he is
involved in an endless conflict between the vision of a "good" life and the
necessity to accommodate oneself to an "evil" world in order to survive. The
impossibility of being "good" in an evil world remains one of the most persistent
themes in Brecht's work from *Die Dreigroschenoper* on ("Ein guter Mensch sein,
ja, wer wär's nicht gern? "), but it is only in these years that Brecht ceases to
"discount" goodness as a luxury, a form of self-indulgence, and to present it as
the desired norm which must not be lost sight of during the "voyage through the
mountains." In the *Flüchtlingsgespräche*[39] Ziffel demonstrates with a good deal
of irony and bitterness how the "virtues" become faults in a society which
exploits them to its own ends, and demands (to quote from the poem "Gleichnis

---

38   GW 9, p. 663
39   GW 14, pp. 1496–7

des Buddha vom brennenden Haus"[40]) that the "Kunst des Duldens" of Buddha and his like should be replaced by a "Kunst des Nicht-Duldens"; but at the same time, there is the recognition that what is really wanted, what must be worked for, is a society where "Dulden" is no longer necessary, where the virtues can be reinstated without involving those who practise them in ruin.

In "An die Nachgeborenen" we are clearly dealing with what we have called a "negative phase" of the dialectic, towards the "lowest point" of 1939, where hope seems to run contrary to all the evidence. If however we ask ourselves where Brecht sees the "positive" phases, in what respect this crisis is in fact not merely a crisis but typical of the view of history and of the world which Brecht has been expounding from the beginning, the argument becomes more complex. For Brecht, all historical times are "finstere Zeiten"; he transfers the "crisis" of the world about him to Rome *(Die Geschäfte des Herrn Julius Cäsar, Das Verhör des Lukullus),* to Grusinien, to Peru, to the Thirty Years' War. Instead of "alienation," we have equivalence: the historical development of the classes is replaced by a timeless and changeless oppression of the "Unteren" by the "Oberen" which finds perhaps its clearest expression in the refrain from "Die Ballade vom Wasserrad" *(Die Rundköpfe und die Spitzköpfe):*

> Freilich dreht das Rad sich immer weiter
> Daß, was oben ist, nicht oben bleibt.
> Aber für das Wasser unten heißt das leider
> Nur: daß es das Rad halt ewig treibt.[41]

This reality of history can only be changed by that revolt of the oppressed which Brecht himself cannot find "natural": its possibility is awaited with an almost religious hope for the "salvation" of mankind. The "finstere Zeiten" become more than the description of a historical phase; they become a characterisation of the "human condition" and the "hope" which Brecht presents comes to have the same non-logical "wish-character" which Ernst Bloch analyses in so many examples of Pre-Marxist literature in *Das Prinzip Hoffnung.*[42] He reverts, in fact, to the antecedents of Marx, to a philosophy which attempts to direct the course of history through the intervention of the consciousness, though aware of the problematic character of this undertaking. Although Brecht himself avoids "Utopias," his "hope" itself has what we might call an "Utopian" character, in that it attempts to transfer the unattainable into the attainable, to reverse the argument of history, which is, as we have seen, to reverse his own earlier argument, to reject the "pessimism" which survives as the "negative" aspect of his new optimism. In "An die Nachgeborenen," the goal is "so far distant" that

---

[40] GW 9, p. 664
[41] GW 3, p. 1007. The anti-technologism of the image is, of course, somewhat unfortunate.
[42] Berlin 1959

Brecht knows that he himself will never reach it, and fears that those who emerge from the "finstere Zeiten" will look back on them with astonishment and, perhaps, lack of understanding. Like Mayakovsky, Brecht finds it hard to visualise a world free of injustice and suffering, not least, because such a society would mean the end of his usefulness (compare the late poem "Der schöne Tag, wenn ich nutzlos geworden bin"[43]), the end of his "mission." He cannot himself belong to this society, just as Mayakovsky's "hero" is "lost" in the "classless" society of The Bed-Bug; and indeed, his art is curiously dependent on the continuation of the "finstere Zeiten" for its effect. Brecht's work is "Arme-Leute-Poesie," it is the literature of the suffering, of the "leidende Kreatur," and it is in this capacity to suffer and yet survive that the real "heroism" of Herr Keuner and Schweijk lies. Here Brecht comes very near to supporting the argument of Friedrich Dürrenmatt, that modern literature can present only the victim, and no longer the hero, as protagonist;[44] the qualities of heroism have become deeply suspect, yet literature, and especially drama, continues to demand a "central character." If he can no longer be distinguished by the high office and great virtues which Aristotle demanded of him, then he may be made relevant by his "sufferings," by his exposure to the unanswerable problems of society, and in this sense, his survival may become a new kind of "heroism." The discrediting of the "sublime" results in a reversion to another and older type of hero, the hero of comedy, the "little man," the Chaplin-figure, whose "qualities" are demonstrated in the exemplary way he accepts and survives his "beatings" from the society in which he lives. Brecht's optimism is that optimism which is available to the "little man," the belief in a vague possibility that some day "things may be different." Chaplin, too, is a survivor, who demonstrates how the "impossible" may be endured and even overcome. The personal "anonymity" which Brecht cultivated is an expression of his desire to survive as the little man, to avoid the exposure of "heroism" and to ally himself rather with the class whose everyday life presented him with a strategy of survival similar to Herr Keuner's, but governed by the dictates of necessity. It is a survival which seems guaranteed by sheer weight of numbers. Yet Brecht's desire to "survive" in "An die Nachgeborenen" in the shape of an eventual emergence of the "good collective" in whose service he has placed himself is not merely a concern for the world and for society, it is at the same time a desire for personal survival through literature. He hopes to escape the "finstere Zeiten" where "die Sprache verriet mich dem Schlächter" and to enjoy "posterity" among those who "emerge" from the flood. Brecht has Odysseus's fear as well as his pride: it is the "nameless" writers whose work has been lost, whose "Wissen" has been wasted, who represent the true "fear" of this last section of the poem.

43   GW 10, p. 1028
44   loc.cit.

The ironic reference to himself as "Klassiker"[45] in these years is only half a joke; it characterises the position of a Laotse, of a Galileo, which he desires for himself but which his society denies him, the "engagement" which would give his work its true function. But the society which Brecht's work wishes to serve does not exist, it is a "far goal," which may or may not choose to preserve and understand the sufferings of Bertolt Brecht in the "finstere Zeiten" of the Twentieth Century.

IV

> Verehrtes Publikum, los, such dir selbst den Schluß:
> Es muß ein guter da sein, muß, muß, muß!
>
> Epilog, *Der gute Mensch von Sezuan*

Der gute Mensch von Sezuan, written between 1938 and 1940, but again not published until after the war, is at once Brecht's most complex and most radical play of the later period. In it the problems which are approached obliquely, even incidentally, in the earlier works are brought out into the open and become the primary concern. More than in any other of the later plays, the plot is subsidiary to the "Aussage:" the dramatic "skin" is thinner than usual. Only in *Die heilige Johanna der Schlachthöfe* and *Der kaukasische Kreidekreis* is a similar direct personal involvement of the author so clearly to be felt.

The parallel with *Johanna* is more than a coincidence; both Johanna and Shen Te are characterised by their "goodness," they are wholly positive figures (despite Johanna's failure to act, which seems almost a consequence of her "goodness"). Both become in the end the victims of an unwilling "canonisation." Johanna's "goodness" is exploited by her enemies for their own ends, Shen Te's is turned by the "gods" into a pitiful excuse for leaving things as they are. Johanna's naivete seems almost a sketch for Shen Te's "natural goodness," and the situation in which Shen Te is placed seems a continuation, a development, of the oppression and suffering of the Chicago stockyards. Both plays are characterised by an extraordinary multiplication of levels of speech. In *Johanna*, we have the blank verse of Mauler, with its classical parody, the language of the Salvation Army, and the spare prose of everyday; in *Der gute Mensch von Sezuan*, the operetta-parody of the gods, the burlesque of Shu Fu, the "heightened speech" of the monologues into which Shen Te so often and so naturally slips, and the earthy and ironic prose of "die Unteren."

There is no character in Brecht's work, with the possible exception of Grusche Vachnadze, who so completely and unambiguously possesses his

---

45 GW 9, p. 559

sympathy as Shen Te. The dilemma of *Mutter Courage* does not arise; the unpleasant qualities which Shen Te eventually finds it necessary to put on in order to survive in the unscrupulous society which surrounds her are transferred to her "other self," Shui Ta, in a manner which makes their "incidental" nature quite clear. Shui Ta is not "characterised," he is merely an unfortunate and "temporarily" necessary function of Shen Te, which she would wish to dispense with completely. There is no attempt to alienate our sympathy from Shen Te herself. We are allowed to pity her, to share her desperate plight at the end of the play in a manner which is quite foreign to *Mutter Courage*. Shen Te, is from the beginning, idealised. Her "instinct,"like Grusche's, is always to do good, but she can expect no freak of history, no Azdak, to save her from the consequences of her actions. Unlike Courage, she hates and despises the means she has to employ in order to survive, her "cousin"; she wants to be only "herself." She experiences the circumstances around her as "unnatural," as forcing her to be someone other than this "self." Like the Brecht of "An die Nachgeborenen," she is in despair at the world's rejection of "goodness," she longs for a society based on "Freundlichkeit," "wo der Mensch dem Menschen ein Helfer ist," and feels her humanity threatened by the surroundings in which she is obliged to exist, her "goodness" exploited and assailed on all sides.

We have seen how Jimmy Mahony's "chorale," "Gegen Verführung," crystallises the attitudes of the early work in its pessimism and its tendency towards an anarchistic self-destruction. In the later plays this "Verführung" to suffering and exploitation is contrasted with a "Verführung zur Güte" (the phrase occurs for the first time in *Der kaukasische Kreidekreis*[46]). We have seen, too, how Johanna's "good qualities" lead to her downfall; they inhibit her capacity to see things as they are, and her charity becomes merely a disastrous self-ilusion, which is rejected firmly in the *Badener Lehrstück,* where "Hilfe" is seen as an error in a world dominated by "Gewalt." Shen Te, too, is ruined by her "goodness," but her "ruin" comes to have a different value. Her failure to solve the problem of "being good and living in the world" does not lead us, as it did in Johanna's case, to condemn her, to accuse her of a lack of insight; Shen Te "kann nicht anders." Her goodness has become a definite positive value in the play. The criticism which had been levelled at the heroine is now directed at the system itself. We are left to draw the conclusion that it must be changed, in order that Shen Te's goodness need no longer involve her in ruin. Brecht is no longer content to assume that the "new society" will produce its own new values, he is now determined not only to "survive" but to plead for the survival of goodness, of "Freundlichkeit." The consciousness of the distance of the goal leads to a new concern with what must happen in the meantime.

46 GW 5, p. 2025

The "good" Shen Te would in fact seem to come from the very beginning of Brecht's world — she is the good which was in the beginning, uncorrupted by the "progress" of civilisation, the state of original unity, a unity which is reflected in the complete naturalness of her actions. Like Evlyn Roe, she is brought into contact with a hostile world which comes between her and her goal, which attempts to corrupt and ruin her. It is hard not to see in the play more than a parable; it is Brecht's own mythology of the "fall," the descent into the "finstere Zeiten" of history. Shen Te is like the "noble savage," presented for the first time with money and unaware of its strange properties. She discovers them to her cost, for at the end of the play her innocence and naivete are lost for ever.

Shen Te comes from a world which anticipates even *Baal*, a world where the virtues are natural, unquestioned and meaningful. She descends into the other world, the world of Mahagonny, and must find an answer to the problem of reconciling the two in order to live. The answer is for her to find, not for the gods; they can offer her no help. To them, her goodness is merely a comforting excuse for abandoning the world; Shen Te cannot and will not exist without it, yet she *must* exist in the world into which she has been flung.

In fact, of course, Shen Te comes from below, not above. She is the classical good-hearted prostitue; like a Dickens heroine she appears "shining bright in the mud." The gods ruin her by the temptation to leave this existence and become a *petit bourgeois,* by offering her "der Rettung kleiner Nachen." She can no longer go back to her earlier life, because in the process of the play she has gained too much insight to be able to be "simply good" again. It is a different insight from Courage's; it is stable and will not change, because it demands a solution as vehemently as the epilogue. But again, it is not a specific insight, like Johanna's. Johanna sees her mistake — Shen Te has made no mistake, even her cousin's actions often do more good than harm, where they are not repealed by her own second thoughts. Johanna would ally herself with the workers, if she had lived; Shen Te is not presented with this alternative — she sees the condition, but not the cure. We fear that she too might make Johanna's "mistake" if it came to the point, whereas Courage, with her greater determination and worldliness, would no doubt have winked at the necessity of "Gewalt."

The situation in which Shen Te finds herself seems, then, to be another expression of the "difficult" optimism of these years, of the consciousness that "Das Ziel lag in großer Ferne" of the period of exile. She is not allowed to reach the stage of Johanna's decision, between clear alternatives; her alternative lies outside the work itself, with the audience. Nevertheless, the play marks a development in Brecht's approach to the problem of the "Marxist drama." While the situation of *Johanna* was particular and critical, Sezuan is possibly Brecht's most extended and successful attempt in all his plays to find a "universal symbol" for the human condition. Despite its Chinoiserie, it generates a "world" which is generalised enough to stand for the society of today and every day. It is the world of what might be called "die kapitalistische Alltagskrise," unexaggerated by the special talents of Pierpont Mauler or by the desolation of the Thirty Years' War. If *Der gute Mensch von Sezuan* seems today perhaps the most important of the later plays, then it is probably because of the "normative" character of the world, and the experience of the world, it represents, the closeness of its perspective, despite its composition in the blackest years of the war, to the present-day scene.

Not that the play is without "problems" — the epilogue alone has provoked a good deal of critical disagreement. But these "problems" seem here to have found their most apposite form, the "question" which we ask ourselves is the question the play itself is asking. The levels at which we respond to *Courage* are here brought together, and the play is built around a recognition of their conflict. The "hidden" problem of *Courage,* whether it is in fact possible to change the world, is here explicit and intentional, and even if it still remains unanswered, we feel that the question has been put in the proper way, that it grows naturally out of the action.

If we are to avoid ignoring what Martin Esslin calls the "Dichotomie zwischen künstlerischer Absicht und tatsächlicher Wirkung"[47] (an entire series of similar dichotomies might be constructed on this model, e.g., "Dichotomie zwischen politischer Absicht und künstlerischer Wirkung," or perhaps even more simply, "zwischen Absicht und Wirkung") we must again ask, not what conclusion Brecht wished to exact from us, but what conclusion we are actually able to draw from the play, since even here Brecht's intention remains somewhat obscure. It is clear that the final scene and epilogue contain the crux of the play, yet many interpretations seem to approach the obvious irony of the epilogue in too naive a manner — it is neither as "negative" as Volker Klotz would have it or as "positive"[48] as Hans Mayer's "gespielte Offenheit." The "openness" of the play is neither merely "gespielt" nor entirely serious; it is, as we have seen, a result of the irony of Herr Keuner, the demonstration of the "hopelessness" of hoping, the "Verhinderung, daß etwas fertig wird" of *Irrtum und Fortschritt*. It is a heavily didactic irony, full of the "politeness" of Herr K., who is not prepared to force his opinion on us, but would be glad to demonstrate that any other is wrong and foolish. Yet the one solution which goes unmentioned, that there might in fact be no solution, is at the same time the source and the result of the irony for those who do not already have an answer. Brecht presents us with a number of wrong solutions, which merely point to the basic question. The "real" solutions, the Marxist and the pessimist, are missing.

---

47 op.cit., p. 311
48 *Bertolt Brecht — Versuch über das Werk*, Darmstadt 1956, pp. 9ff.

This covering irony is present throughout the play in the person of the three "gods," whose basic failure to appreciate the seriousness of the situation is used consciously by Brecht to counterbalance the unrelieved difficulty of Shen Te's position. Whether these gods are borrowed, as Mayer claims, from the early poem "Matinee in Dresden"[49] or whether they represent merely the three wise monkeys of the Benares temple, they have no power and no understanding and are reduced to the function of comic relief. Shen Te's protest is not really addressed to them, just as the solutions of the epilogue are facetious; the audience is never in doubt that the appeal is being made to them, not to these comic and pathetic comrades in divinity.

In *Der gute Mensch von Sezuan* Brecht employs a device which effectively prevents the ambivalence of *Mutter Courage* — the direct appeal to the public, no longer merely an "Aus-der-Rolle-Fallen," a "Verfremdungseffekt," but a deliberate and serious use of the straight emotive appeal which he had previously tended to reject with some violence. When She Te addresses the audience, there is none of the ambiguity of Courage's precepts, none of the fear of becoming "kenntlich," of exposing herself, which lies behind Courage's actions. It is clear that the author is speaking his mind "through" her, as if he had at last found the right mouthpiece to speak the "truth." The step which is demanded of us at the end of the play becomes an easier step, because Shen Te is so clearly an "apostle of the future." We can glimpse the "Ziel" in her speeches, even if we are told little of how to get there. The "wish-character" of Brecht's Marxism is nowhere clearer than here: the three-fold "muß" of the epilogue is an appeal for hope in a situation which seems utterly hopeless, but which by this very hopelessness seems to demand an end and, perhaps, a new beginning. Shen Te, as mother, demands a new world for her son; it is the thought of the future which forces her into consciousness and action.

Herr Keuner seems to have thrown caution to the winds, at least temporarily. No where else in his whole work does he deliver his "Nein" so clearly and vigorously, no where else does he show this particular variety of moral courage, this willingness to "expose" himself. It is as if Laotse had determined that his "wisdom" should not be lost before he leaves the country; he no longer waits for it to be "extracted" from him. Shen Te is not afraid, as Brecht's other heroines (except Grusche) are afraid; she has the unquestioned goodness and certainty of action of Kattrin in *Mutter Courage,* but it is no longer merely a "dumb" goodness. She becomes the clearest and most direct of all his "Neinsager."

More than *Kreidekreis,* where goodness is dependent on accident for its survival, where the "fairy-tale" becomes the image of hope, *Der gute Mensch von Sezuan* represents the farthest point in Brecht's search for a dramatic form which will plead the necessity of change to the audience, will show them in the

49 Mayer, *Ansichten,* p. 103

present the embryo of a possible future society as a "natural" human goodness,
which is still possible, even if it places those who practise it in an intolerable
position. Without contravening Brecht's fundamental principle of "realism," this
form becomes more than "realistic," it expresses the wish as well as the reality,
the "Fortschritt" as well as the "Irrtum." If we are unable to "deduce" Marxism
from the play, then at least there are few of us who would reject the play's
analysis of contemporary society and the "muß" of the epilogue. The plea for an
attempt to transform the "hopelessness," to change the intolerable, is nowhere
stronger; to answer Shen Te with our pessimism seems a betrayal, not merely of
goodness, but of humanity.

V

Und nach diesem Abend verschwand der Azdak und ward nicht mehr
gesehen.
Aber das Volk Grusiniens vergaß ihn nicht und gedachte noch
Lange seiner Richterzeit als einer kurzen
Goldenen Zeit beinahe der Gerechtigkeit.
                    Der kaukasische Kreidekreis, Schlußszene[50]

Es ist unmöglich, das Glücksverlangen der Menschen ganz zu töten.
                              Bei Durchsicht meiner ersten Stücke[51]

   That Brecht in *Der kaukasische Kreidekreis* should finally have succeeded
(quite seriously) in producing a "happy ending" must astonish any reader
familiar with the barrage of satire which he had directed against such "false
Utopias" from *Baal* onwards. *Die Dreigroschenoper*, with its "reitender Bote," is
the prime example of Brecht's deep-rooted cynicism on the subject of "chance"
intervening to save the "deserving." "Chance" has no place either in the negative
dialectic of the earlier work nor in the Marxist world-picture of the later plays; it
is a fraudulent attempt to interfere with the workings of history, whether their
direction is negative or eventually positive. So many of Brecht's views might be
prefaced with the classical Marxist "Es ist kein Zufall, daß . . . ," that it comes as
a tremendous surprise to find him invoking chance himself in order to re-unite
Grusche Vachnadze with her lover Simon and to give the question of the child's
parentage a solution which the reader well knows it could never find "in real
life."
   Büchner's Lenz, in the depths of his suffering, complains to Oberlin: "Aber
ich, wär ich allmächtig, sehen Sie, wenn ich so wäre, ich könnte das Leiden nicht

50   GW 5, p. 2105
51   GW 17, p. 948

ertragen, ich würde retten, retten."[52], In *Der kaukasische Kreidekreis*, this desire to "rescue" humanity from its endless struggle against injustice and oppression, to present virtue with its reward "here and now," gets the better, for once, of Brecht's restraint, and he intervenes to suspend the inexorable logic by which goodness leads to ruin. Azdak's justice is an attempt to subvert "the way of the world," to make the impossible happen through exploiting a chance constellation of circumstances. The "Wechsel der Zeiten" which forms the background of the play, the uneasy interregnum where the fat prince is still dependent on the whims of his soldiers, where chaos makes the unforeseen possible, provides the apparent justification for this unusual outcome; yet, at the same time, Brecht is concerned throughout to stress its "exceptional quality," the fact that "things just don't happen this way," no doubt partly as a sop to his own artistic conscience. The "Märchen" is the literary form we might well assume to have been the least attractive to Brecht, yet in *Kreidekreis* he comes very close to creating a "fairy-tale" of his own. The care with which it is embedded in a prosaic "Rahmen" does not really conceal the fact that it is Brecht's desire to intervene, for once, in the person of Azdak and alter the course of society to save Grusche's goodness which is the real *raison d'être* of the play, and not the weighty problem raised in the prologue.

The "happy ending" of *Kreidekreis* changes nothing. After Azdak's departure, things will return to normal; Grusche and Simon will be in danger of their lives and of losing the child. Characteristically the return to normality is symbolised by the restoration of the "Großfürst"; the "Wasserrad" has returned to its point of origin. Azdak's cunning and Grusche's goodness, then, have little hope of success in the world outside the play; the extraordinary and atypical triumph they achieve in a moment "outside history" has value only in the hope it conveys for the future and in the moral satisfaction it gives reader and, more importantly still, author.

In the person of Azdak, Brecht/Keuner finally comes to the aid of his suffering heroines; his strategy of survival finds its justification not in that survival alone, but in the way he is able to employ his "Wissen" in the face of adversity to achieve "eine kurze goldene Zeit beinah der Gerechtigkeit." Although his character is at least as "flawed" as Galileo's, he is prepared to run risks for others which stand in some conflict with his Schweijkian cunning; this becomes clearest in his rescue of Grusche, which is scarcely calculated to ensure his own personal safety. Yet, typically enough, Azdak "disappears" after the play has reached its apparent resolution; he has returned to the safe anonymity from which he had temporarily and uncharacteristically emerged.

Not that Grusche is in any sense a "hilfloser Knabe"; it is her courage and resourcefulness, her "active" goodness which seems to demand Azdak's

52 *Werke und Briefe*, p. 109

intervention, if his survival is not to become a meaningless exile. The polarity
Kattrin/Courage is rejected in *Kreidekreis;* although Brecht is not averse to
stressing Grusche's "stupidity," her lack of Keunerian "List" and her naive
acceptance of the dangers of "goodness," the play does not finally support these
judgments. Grusche, like Shen Te, "kann nicht anders," and this is the real
source of her strength and of the reluctant admiration she inspires in Azdak and
his creator. Azdak's "Flucht nach vorn," his acceptance of the dangerous role of
"Richter," is, in the last analysis, an attempt to prove that his "Wissen" is as
valuable a contribution to social change as Grusche's resoluteness and the direct
action of "Sankt Banditus."[53] If his self-accusation, which leads to the whole
development, is at first only an ingenious attempt to circumvent the full severity
of the penalty to which he has exposed himself by harbouring the "Großfürst,"
his continuation in the position of judge is far more than an "Ausweg," and his
venality, for all its comic effect, seems more of a shamefaced attempt on the
part of a writer who admitted "[daß] ich ein schlechter Esser bin"[54] to balance
the element of courage and self-exposure involved by adopting a comic mask.

It is required, too, to balance the tone of the Grusche action, which employs
a more lyrical and emotive diction than Brecht had attempted for years. Already
in *Der gute Mensch von Sezuan* he had, with uncharacteristic lack of reserve,
come dangerously close to the brink of sentimentality, yet the ingenious device
of Shen Te's "split personality" and the multiple levels of the play provide a
counterweight. In the first part of *Kreidekreis,* this balance is largely lacking (as
a result of its binary structure), and Azdak's combination of vice and wit comes
as something of a relief. It is, no doubt, significant that even in this, his most
forthright play, Brecht should have clung to the stylised distinction between
simple goodness (found only, it seems, in proletarian females) and amoral
cleverness (a characteristic of male intellectuals!). Grusche quite rightly senses an
element of condescension in Azdak's treatment of her, and if Azdak enjoys her
recriminations, it is perhaps because he recognises their justice.

The characterisation of Azdak is the farthest development of the Keuner
figure in Brecht's work, yet for all the apparent gaiety of the play, it solves few
of the inherent problems. In *Kreidekreis,* Brecht was not content to remain in
the negative phase of *Mutter Courage* and *An die Nachgeborenen;* in 1944–5,
when the play was written, he may indeed have found it possible to look at the
immediate future with a glimmering of optimism. Temporarily, at least, it must
have looked to him as if the long-awaited return, the "aus niemals wird heute
noch," was in sight and that it might mean a return to a new and better
Germany. Yet the "solution" of *Kreidekreis* is of such a kind that it makes clear
to us why this solution is missing elsewhere; it is the result of impatience rather

53   GW 5, p. 2084
54   GW 10, p. 1031

than conviction, a desire to see the good succeed for once, rather than the belief that such a success is imminent or even probable.

The impatience of *Kreidekreis* is a mirror image of the "pessimistic impatience" we have analysed in the early work, a desire to hasten the progression of the dialectic towards its limit, to bring "niemals" within the reach of "heute," so that the weary passenger, Baal/Keuner, can dismount. Just as the early Brecht, having established that the apocalypse is near, tries to hasten the end, so the later Brecht yearns for the Utopian end of history to come close enough to grasp, or at least to see. However convinced he may be that the "Glücksverlangen" of humanity is indestructible and that "one day" ("one day" becomes an expression of bitterness in the last poems[55]) it will succeed in forming society for the good of all, this helps him little to survive the present which fills his plays and poems, the "finstere Zeit" where friendliness is impossible. *Kreidekreis* is the expression of this wish to be released from the relentless and unending progression of the dialectic, to be allowed to enjoy some of the fruits of "Freundlichkeit" in the present itself.

It was surely with this impatience that Brecht greeted the end of the war and the prospect of return to Germany. It is an optimism which survives briefly in the first years, but which, like Laotse's, is fated to see that "die Bosheit nahm an Kräften wieder zu," an optimism which for a while attempts to free itself from its own better knowledge that "das Ziel lag in großer Ferne," but is forced to realise that this "Wechsel der Zeiten" has again disappointed "die Hoffnung des Volks."[56] For all the softening of Herr K.'s attitudes, the time is not yet ripe for him to emerge from anonymity: the real, the decisive change still withholds itself.

VI

> Dauerten wir unendlich
> So wandelte sich alles
> Da wir aber endlich sind
> Bleibt vieles beim alten.[57]

In *Der gute Mensch von Sezuan* and *Der kaukasische Kreidekreis* Brecht achieves the climax of his work — the two plays represent a degree of positivity, of eloquence and directness which convince us that the difficulties of the thirties have been worthwhile, that Brecht has finally found his way back to the

---

55 cf. GW 10, p. 1027
56 GW 5, p. 2015
57 GW 10, p. 1031

"personality" which he has been attempting to eliminate from his work and has attained a new breadth and universality. Yet it is a climax, a high point, which he is forced to abandon. The balance of hope and hopelessness which marks Shen Te's last speech and the epilogue in *Der gute Mensch von Sezuan* cannot be maintained against a pessimism which is obliged by its insight into the world around to reassert itself. Brecht's optimism remains an "effort," it has continually to confront itself with a reality which does not seem to support it.

The poems of the last years are characterised by a weariness, a realisation that the world has not changed as he would wish it to have, but that every advance must be "erstrebt und erkämpft" with enormous difficulty, since the old tends to re-appear and to oppose the new. The "unending" nature of the dialectic is now no longer a proof of the possibility of hope, it becomes rather the experience that one man can himself witness so little progress that his end and his beginning seem close together, the years between have changed only the form of the "finstere Zeiten," but not their character. Many of the poems are reflections of this realisation that things are "wie in alten Zeiten,"[58] that the change which has come has been minimal. The Brecht of *Mahagonny* has grown old, but his essential unrest remains unchanged, his conviction that "etwas fehlt":

> Ich bin nicht gern, wo ich herkomme.
> Ich bin nicht gern, wo ich hinfahre.
> Warum sehe ich den Radwechsel
> Mit Ungeduld? [59]

Yet the pessimism of *Der Radwechsel* is not without hope — the "Ungeduld" with which he watches this operation is an unbroken belief that from this "choice of evils" the good may yet result. Martin Esslin relates a parable which Brecht is said to have used to explain this "hope" in the last years:

> Ein Arzt in einem Krankenhaus steht zwei gleichermaßen mit einer ekelerregenden Geschlechtskrankheit behafteten Patienten gegenüber — einem alten Lebemann und einer schwangeren Straßendirne. Er hat aber nur so viel Penizillin zur Verfügung, um einen von diesen beiden Patienten zu retten. Wird er nicht das Mädchen retten müssen, weil doch bei ihr zumindest die Chance besteht, daß sie ein gesundes Kind in die Welt setzen wird? [60]

The "optimism" of the *Buckower Elegien* is of a similar kind; it is an optimism which hopes only because the alternative means the destruction of all hope. In one of the very latest poems Brecht allows himself a directness which is very uncharacteristic of his work:

58 GW 10, p. 1011
59 GW 10, p. 1009
60 op.cit., p. 270

War traurig, wann ich jung war
Bin traurig, nun ich alt
So, wann kann ich mal lustig sein?
Es wäre besser bald.[61]

The memory of Augsburg becomes dominant ("Heißer Tag,"[62] "Schwierige Zeiten,"[63] "Tannen"[64]); two world wars and fifty years have not sufficed to "teach" the world its error, and Brecht, like Laotse, finds himself no further. The overriding question of these last poems becomes: has the effort been useless? Have I failed to change the world, as I set out to do in the thirties? One of the most important documents of these years is Brecht's reply to a question raised by Friedrich Dürrenmatt, "Kann die heutige Welt durch Theater wiedergegeben werden?." For Brecht, this question is so basic that it involves an exposition of the whole "problem" of an optimism which may seem to be against the facts:

> Es wird Sie nicht verwundern, von mir zu hören, daß die Frage der Beschreibbarkeit der Welt eine gesellschaftliche Frage ist. Ich habe diese viele Jahre lang aufrechterhalten und lebe jetzt in einem Staat, wo eine ungeheure Anstrengung gemacht wird, die Gesellschaft zu verändern. Sie mögen die Mittel und Wege verurteilen — ich hoffe übrigens, Sie kennen sie wirklich, nicht aus den Zeitungen —, Sie mögen dieses besondere Ideal einer neuen Welt nicht akzeptieren — ich hoffe, Sie kennen auch dieses —, aber Sie werden kaum bezweifeln, daß an der Änderung der Welt, des Zusammenlebens der Menschen in dem Staat, in dem ich lebe, gearbeitet wird. Und Sie werden mir vielleicht darin zustimmen, daß die heutige Welt eine Änderung braucht.[65]

We have seen that it was this possibility of change, this possibility of an "escape" from the "finstere Zeiten" which Brecht had characterised once and for all in *Mahagonny* and which remain the backdrop against which his work is played out, which became for Brecht synonymous with the possibility of "surviving," continuing in the hope of a better world; it is this hope alone which gives meaning to the long servitude of Herr Egge, which can release Shen Te from the strange schizophrenia the world inflicts on her. To deny the possibility of change, or more specifically, to deny the possibility of "changing," is to destroy the construction on which Brecht's entire later work is based, to reduce him to Dürrenmatt's own pessimism, which claims that the author can in fact only change the world on stage, that his fine desire to change the world results only in an aesthetic distortion of it. In the midst of the theatrical triumphs of these

61 GW 10, p. 1030
62 GW 10, p. 1011
63 GW 10, p. 1029
64 GW 10, p. 1012
65 GW 16, pp. 930–1

years, Brecht's poems give an insight into the true misgiving with which he had
come to regard his "success" — the Berliner Ensemble had become in its way a
small and perfect paradigm of the Marxist society, but the world itself was as far
as ever from achieving it. The "unchanging" quality of the last verse is for Brecht
a very depressive note indeed, since it is only change that makes hope possible.
He has failed to weather the storm because the storm has outlasted him, his
retreat into anonymity has not saved him, since the collective of "no-ones"
which should have absorbed his single failure delays its appearance, and he is no
longer content to remain "no-one" without this hope, since this is no more than
the self-destruction of the early period. In the end, his identity is a burden, a
reminder of the unchanged past which makes the same claims on him that it had
made in the early years. To quote once more Klaus Heinrich's interpretation of
the *Keunergeschichte* "Das Wiedersehen":

> Er ist ertappt als Nicht-Keiner. Er trägt seine Identität als eine Last mit sich
> herum und kann sie nicht loswerden: sie hat ihn verraten.[66]

He is caught between the desire to see the realisation of his own wishes, to step
out into the open as one who has "survived" and the realisation that the danger,
the "storm," is not yet past. He is tired of "die Schwierigkeiten des Niemand"
and wishes to become "kenntlich" once more, yet he has not found the
possibility.

Even the reconcilement of one of his very last poems, "Als ich in weißem
Krankenzimmer der Charité,"[67] where the *Mahagonny*-like recognition that
death will release him from the "aber etwas fehlt" which has accompanied him
for so many years is turned "positive" by the thought that the "blackbirds" will
continue to sing when he is gone (in the poem "Die Vögel warten im Winter vor
dem Fenster"[68] the blackbird comes to stand for the artist, whose "song" is also
work) is a far cry from the world that Shen Te heralded; the "good" may
survive, but perhaps never break through the oppression of the "finstere Zeiten."
Yet this hope still remains for the dying Brecht, and it is enough.

66   op.cit., p. 52
67   GW 10, p. 1031
68   GW 10, p. 971

BIBLIOGRAPHY

Listed here are only those works referred to *directly* in the text. For a detailed bibliography the reader is referred to the latest edition of Reinhold Grimm's *Bertolt Brecht* in the Sammlung Metzler.

A. Texts

Gesammelte Werke, 20 vols., Frankfurt 1967 (= GW)
Aufstieg und Fall der Stadt Mahagonny, Oper von Kurt Weill, Text von Brecht, Wien 1929
Baal. Drei Fassungen, ed. D. Schmidt, Frankfurt 1966
Baal. Der böse Baal der asoziale. Texte, Varianten, Materialien, ed. D. Schmidt, Frankfurt 1968
Gedichte 1—9, Frankfurt 1960—66
Stücke 1—14, Frankfurt 1953—66
Gerhard Szczesny, *Das Leben des Galileo und der Fall Bertolt Brecht*, Berlin 1966 (contains Scenes 8, 9 and 13 of the first version)
Versuche 1—4, reprinted Frankfurt 1959

B. Collections

Bertolt Brechts Dreigroschenbuch, Frankfurt 1960
Demetz, P., ed., *Brecht. A Collection of Critical Essays*, Englewood Cliffs 1963
Materialien zu Brechts "Leben des Galilei," Frankfurt 1967
Sinn und Form, 2. Sonderheft Bertolt Brecht, Berlin 1957

C. Critical Works

Adorno, T. W., *Moments Musicaux*, Frankfurt 1964
Benjamin, W., *Illuminationen*, Frankfurt 1961
Benjamin W., *Versuche über Brecht*, Frankfurt 1966
Bloch, E., *Erbschaft dieser Zeit*, Frankfurt 1962
Blume, B., "Motive der frühen Lyrik Brechts," *Monatshefte* LVII (1965), pp. 96ff. and 273ff.
Bronnen, A., *Tage mit Bert Brecht*, Munich 1960
Chambers, R., "Beckett's Brinkmanship," *AUMLA* 19 (May 1963), pp. 57ff.
Drew, D., "The History of Mahagonny," *Musical Times* 1963/1, pp. 18ff.
Dürrenmatt, F., *Theaterprobleme*, Zurich 1955
Esslin, M., *Brecht. Das Paradox des politischen Dichters*, Frankfurt 1962
Fülleborn, U., "Form und Sinn der *Aufzeichnungen des Malte Laurids Brigge*," *Unterscheidung und Bewahrung*, Festschrift für Hermann Kunisch, Berlin 1961, pp. 147ff.
Heinrich, K., *Versuch über die Schwierigkeit nein zu sagen*, Frankfurt 1964
Herzfeld, F., *Musica Nova*, Berlin 1954
Hinck, W., *Die Dramaturgie des späten Brecht*, Göttingen 1959
Hultberg, H., *Die ästhetischen Anschauungen Bertolt Brechts*, Copenhagen 1962
Kesting, M., "Die Groteske vom Verlust der Identität: Bertolt Brechts *Mann ist Mann*," *Das deutsche Lustspiel* II. Teil, ed. H. Steffen, Göttingen 1970, pp. 180ff.
Klotz, V., *Bertolt Brecht, Versuch über das Werk*, Darmstadt 1956
Martens, W., "Ideologie und Verzweiflung. Religiöse Motive in Büchners Revolutionsdrama," *Euphorion* 54 (1960), pp. 83ff.
Mayer, H., *Ansichten*, Hamburg 1962

Mayer, H., "Berliner Dramaturgie von Gerhart Hauptmann bis Peter Weiss," *Theater heute* 12 (1965), pp. 1ff.

Mayer, H., *Bertolt Brecht und die Tradition*, Pfullingen 1961

Mayer, H., *Studien*, Berlin 1955

Melchinger, S., "Mahagonny als Mysterienspiel," *Theater heute* Mai 1964, pp. 32ff.

Münsterer, H. O., *Bert Brecht. Erinnerungen aus den Jahren 1917—22*, Zurich 1963

Schmidt, D., *"Baal" und der junge Brecht*, Stuttgart 1966

Schuhmacher, E., *Die dramatischen Versuche Bertolt Brechts 1918—1933*, Berlin 1955

Schuhmacher, E., *Drama und Geschichte. Leben des Galilei und andere Stücke*, Berlin 1965

Steinweg, R., *Brechts Lehrstück. Untersuchung eines Theorie-Praxis Modells*, Diss., Kiel 1969

Steinweg, R., *Das Lehrstück. Brechts Theorie einer politisch-ästhetischen Erziehung*, Stuttgart 1971

Sternberg, F., *Der Dichter und die Ratio*, Göttingen 1963

Szondi, P., *Theorie des modernen Dramas*, Frankfurt 1959

Wekwerth, M., *Theater in Veränderung*, Berlin 1960

D. Recordings

Aufstieg und Fall der Stadt Mahagonny, Philips L09418—20L

Lotte Lenya sings Berlin Theatre Songs, CBS KLC507